First World War
and Army of Occupation
War Diary
France, Belgium and Germany

58 DIVISION
Divisional Troops
Suffolk Regiment
4th Battalion Pioneers
1 February 1916 - 31 July 1919

WO95/2996/9

The Naval & Military Press Ltd
www.nmarchive.com
Published in association with The National Archives

Published by

The Naval & Military Press Ltd

Unit 10 Ridgewood Industrial Park,

Uckfield, East Sussex,

TN22 5QE England

Tel: +44 (0) 1825 749494

www.naval-military-press.com

www.nmarchive.com

This diary has been reprinted in facsimile from the original. Any imperfections are inevitably reproduced and the quality may fall short of modern type and cartographic standards.

© **Crown Copyright**
Images reproduced by permission of The National Archives, London, England, 2015.

Contents

Document type	Place/Title	Date From	Date To
Heading	WO95/2996/9		
Heading	58th Division 1-4th Bn Suffolk Regt (Pioneers) 1918 Feb-1919 Jly From 33Div 98Bde		
War Diary	Noir Carme	01/02/1916	11/02/1916
War Diary	Renescure	12/02/1916	14/02/1916
War Diary	Appilly	15/02/1916	15/02/1916
War Diary	Rouez Camp	16/02/1916	24/02/1916
War Diary	Chauny	25/02/1916	25/02/1916
War Diary	Bichancourt	26/02/1916	24/03/1916
War Diary	Besme	25/03/1916	25/03/1916
War Diary	Pierremande	26/03/1916	26/03/1916
War Diary	St Paul Aux Bois	27/03/1916	31/03/1916
Heading	War Diary 1/4th Battn. The Suffolk Regiment April 1918		
Miscellaneous	Messages And Signals		
War Diary	St Paul Aux Bois	01/04/1918	03/04/1918
War Diary	Le Mesnil	04/04/1918	04/04/1918
War Diary	St Pierre-Aigle	05/04/1918	06/04/1918
War Diary	Trenches	07/04/1918	30/04/1918
Miscellaneous	A Form Messages And Signals		
War Diary	Maison Rolland	01/05/1918	07/05/1918
War Diary	Wood S.E. of Moliens Au Bois	08/05/1918	08/05/1918
War Diary	Bois Robert	09/05/1918	17/05/1918
War Diary	Trenches Near Henencourt	18/05/1918	31/05/1918
Miscellaneous	58th Division	09/07/1918	09/07/1918
War Diary	N. Of Baizieux	01/06/1918	05/06/1918
War Diary	N. Of Beaucourt	06/06/1918	10/06/1918
War Diary	Crouy	11/06/1918	17/06/1918
War Diary	Trenches	18/06/1918	30/06/1918
Miscellaneous	Headquarters 58th Division		
War Diary	Trenches	01/07/1918	31/07/1918
Heading	4th Battalion Suffolk Regiment (Pioneers) August 1918		
War Diary	Trenches	01/08/1918	02/08/1918
War Diary	Bois Robert	03/08/1918	03/08/1918
War Diary	Villers Bocage	04/08/1918	05/08/1918
War Diary	Bois Escardonneuse	06/08/1918	07/08/1918
War Diary	Trenches	08/08/1918	08/08/1918
War Diary	N. Of Sailly Laurette	09/08/1918	10/08/1918
War Diary	Bois Escardonneuse	11/08/1918	11/08/1918
War Diary	N. Of Sailly Laurette	12/08/1918	13/08/1918
War Diary	Bois Escardonneuse	14/08/1918	24/08/1918
War Diary	West Of Bois de Tailles	25/08/1918	28/08/1918
War Diary	Bois D'en Haut	29/08/1918	29/08/1918
War Diary	S Of Maurepas	30/08/1918	30/08/1918
War Diary	S Of Hospital Wood	31/08/1918	31/08/1918
War Diary	S Of Maricourt	01/09/1918	06/09/1918
War Diary	Rancourt	07/09/1918	07/09/1918
War Diary	E Of Moislains	08/09/1918	08/09/1918
War Diary	S Of Nurlu	09/09/1918	10/09/1918
War Diary	Trenches	11/09/1918	11/09/1918

War Diary	S. Of Nurlu	12/09/1918	14/09/1918
War Diary	Trenches	15/09/1918	16/09/1918
War Diary	S. Of Nurlu	17/09/1918	20/09/1918
War Diary	Trenches	21/09/1918	23/09/1918
War Diary	Bricqueterie Camp	24/09/1918	26/09/1918
War Diary	Train	27/09/1918	27/09/1918
War Diary	Camp S Of Hersin	28/09/1918	28/09/1918
War Diary	S Of Hersin	29/09/1918	29/09/1918
War Diary	Maroc	30/09/1918	03/10/1918
War Diary	Cite St Pierre	04/10/1918	05/10/1918
Miscellaneous	Herewith War Diary Of This Battalion For October 1918	08/11/1918	08/11/1918
War Diary	Cite St. Pierre	06/10/1918	15/10/1918
War Diary	Harnes	16/10/1918	17/10/1918
War Diary	Courriers	18/10/1918	18/10/1918
War Diary	Ostricourt	19/10/1918	19/10/1918
War Diary	Mons En Pevele	20/10/1918	20/10/1918
War Diary	Auchy	21/10/1918	22/10/1918
War Diary	Aix	23/10/1918	26/10/1918
War Diary	Rongy	27/10/1918	31/10/1918
Miscellaneous	Herewith Original War Diary For The Month Of November 1918	02/12/1918	02/12/1918
War Diary	Rongy	01/11/1918	09/11/1918
War Diary	Rouex	10/11/1918	10/11/1918
War Diary	Wiers	11/11/1918	11/11/1918
War Diary	Basecles	12/11/1918	14/11/1918
War Diary	Ecacheries	15/11/1918	30/11/1918
Miscellaneous	Herewith War Diary Of This Battalion For December 1918	06/01/1919	06/01/1919
War Diary	Ecacheries	01/12/1918	19/12/1918
War Diary	Stambruges	20/12/1918	31/12/1918
Miscellaneous	Herewith War Diary Of This Battalion For January 1919	12/02/1919	12/02/1919
War Diary	Stambruges	01/01/1919	28/02/1919
Heading	Rhine Army Eastern Division (Late 34th Division) 4th Bn Suffolk Regiment Mar-Jly 1919		
War Diary	Stambruges	01/03/1919	02/03/1919
War Diary	Leuze	03/03/1919	04/03/1919
War Diary	Troisdorf	05/03/1919	31/03/1919
Miscellaneous	Herewith War Diary Of This Battalion For April 1919		
War Diary	Troisdorf (Cologne)	01/04/1919	09/04/1919
War Diary	Troisdorf	10/04/1919	31/05/1919
Miscellaneous	Battalion Orders by Lieutenant Colonel G.C. Stubbs D.S.O. Commanding 4th Battalion Suffolk Regiment in the Field	25/05/1919	25/05/1919
War Diary	Troisdorf	01/06/1919	18/06/1919
War Diary	Heister	19/06/1919	30/06/1919
War Diary	Troisdorf	01/07/1919	31/07/1919

WO 95/29969

58TH DIVISION

1-4TH BN SUFFOLK REGT.
(PIONEERS)
~~FEB 1918 - FEB 1919~~

1918 FEB — 1919 JLY

FROM 33 DIV 98 BDE

WAR DIARY
or
INTELLIGENCE SUMMARY.   1/4th SUFFOLK REGT

(Erase heading not required.)

Army Form C. 2118.

Place	Date	Hour	Summary of Events and Information	Remarks and references to Appendices
NOIR CARME	Feb 1st		Companies at disposal of company commanders	F.P.
NOIR CARME	Feb 2nd		Company parades & inspection	F.P.
NOIR CARME	Feb 3rd		Church service in village school room 11.30 A.M	F.P.
NOIR CARME	Feb 4th		All ranks attended a lecture by Brigade Gas Officer. A & B Companies on rifle range during afternoon	F.P.
NOIR CARME	Feb 5th		Company training during morning. Company Arms & football in the afternoon.	F.P.
NOIR CARME	Feb 6th		Company training. Battalion cinema in evening	F.P.
NOIR CARME	Feb 7th		Weather became wet & intspersed with rit-down work. Battalion cinema in evening 200436 PTE H. GARDINER was awarded the Belgium Croix de Guerre.	F.P.

R. Greener Lt Col

Army Form C. 2118.

WAR DIARY
or
INTELLIGENCE SUMMARY. 1/4TH SUFFOLK REGT

(Erase heading not required.)

Instructions regarding War Diaries and Intelligence Summaries are contained in F. S. Regs., Part II. and the Staff Manual respectively. Title pages will be prepared in manuscript.

Place	Date	Hour	Summary of Events and Information	Remarks and references to Appendices
NOIR CARME	Feb 8TH		Weather continued wet. Baths were allotted to the battalion.	
			A letter was received from Sir Arthur Lawley expressing appreciation for the subscription sent by the regiment to the funds of the Red Cross.	T.P.
			The following officers joined the battalion :- 2ND LIEUT (A/CAPT) N. BOLINGBROKE, 1ST & 2ND LIEUTS H.H. WEBB, E.W. ASTILL, E.R. KIRBY, H. PITCHFORD, J.W. JORDAN also 203 O.R. M.O. D.C.M.	
NOIR	Feb 9TH		Training continued in morning	T.P.
CARME			3 O.R. joined the battalion	
NOIR	Feb 10TH		Church service in the morning	
CARME			In the afternoon at 2.30. a cross country run for teams from each unit in the brigade took place. Three teams each consisting of 10 runners entered & the event was won by 1st Bn Middlesex Regt with our team a good second. The battalion was represented by C.Q.M.S. Green, S/Sgt C.Q.M.S. Rhoades, Sergt Clarke, Corpl Green, Whitton & Chambers, L/Corpls Naylor & Cowell & Ptes Barker & Catchpole. Ptes Catchpole, Laurie & Sergt Clarke secured 1st, 2nd & 4th individual prizes in addition to the	T.P.

Army Form C. 2118.

Army Form C. 2118.

WAR DIARY
or
INTELLIGENCE SUMMARY.
(Erase heading not required.)

1/4th SUFFOLK R E67

Place	Date	Hour	Summary of Events and Information	Remarks and references to Appendices
	Feb. 10th (cont.)		Large satchels presented to each member of the team. Prizes were presented by Brigadier General Heriott Maitland commanding 98th Inf Bde.	
NOIR CARME	Feb 11th		Battalion paraded + left NOIR CARME at 8.30 to take over duties of a Pioneer Battalion to another division. Brigadier-General Heriott Maitland + staff of the 98th Infy Bde were at the starting point to see us off + any "God Speed" by the Band + Drums of the 1st Bn Middlesex Regt + 4th Bn King's Liverpool Regt + the Pipers of the 2nd Bn Argyll + Sutherland Highlanders were kindly sent by Commanding Officers to play us on our way, a courtesy much appreciated by all ranks of the 4th Suffolks. We left the 98th Bde + 33rd Division (with which we had served since March 1st 1916) with regret + judging by expression of friendship received from all ranks this was mutual. Reached RENESCURE at 12.45 P.M. + went into billets.	7P

Army Form C. 2118.

WAR DIARY
or
INTELLIGENCE SUMMARY. 1/4th SUFFOLK REGT
(Erase heading not required.)

Instructions regarding War Diaries and Intelligence Summaries are contained in F. S. Regs., Part II. and the Staff Manual respectively. Title pages will be prepared in manuscript.

Place	Date	Hour	Summary of Events and Information	Remarks and references to Appendices
RENESCURE	Feb 12th		Paraded at 8.30 A.M for inspection by Major General J R Pinney C.B. commanding 33rd division. In a short address at the conclusion of the inspection the Divisional Commander expressed his appreciation of the work done by the regiment during the time it was in his command & his regret at losing it.	J.P
RENESCURE	Feb 13th		Weather wet. Preparations made to move by train at short notice	
RENESCURE	Feb 14th		Transport moved at 6.30 & the battalion marched at 8 A.M to BAVINCHOVE (near CASSEL) & entrained. Train started at 1.30 P.M & train detraining station APPILLY was reached at 4 A.M on 15th Feb.	J.P
APPILLY	Feb 15th		Arrived at APPILLY 4 A.M & marched to MAREST where we rested till 2 P.M & then marched to ROUEZ & were accommodated in a camp in ROUEZ WOOD. Here we came under the orders of the 58th Division – 3rd Corps – 5th Army. Very cold night. "D" Coy detached to VIRY=NOREUIL.	J.P

M Grocers ALC

Army Form C. 2118.

WAR DIARY
or
INTELLIGENCE SUMMARY.   1/4th SUFFOLK REGT

(Erase heading not required.)

Instructions regarding War Diaries and Intelligence
Summaries are contained in F. S. Regs., Part II.
and the Staff Manual respectively. Title pages
will be prepared in manuscript.

Place	Date	Hour	Summary of Events and Information	Remarks and references to Appendices
ROUEZ CAMP	Feb 16th		Furnished working party numbering 150 for work at Divisional H.Q. Remainder cleaning up & improving ROUEZ CAMP. Beautiful weather.	7.P.
ROUEZ CAMP	Feb 17th		Furnished working party of 150 for work at Divisional H.Q. Remainder baths & improving camp. Officers reconnoitred forward area.	7.P.
ROUEZ CAMP	Feb 18th		Working party of 150 for work at Divisional H.Q. Remainder baths & improving camp. "D" Coy moved from VIRY to AUTRVILLE	7.P.
ROUEZ CAMP	Feb 19th		Working party of 150 at Div H.Q.; "D" Coy at work on Southern area. Remainder baths & camp improvements.	7.P.
ROUEZ CAMP	Feb 20th		Working party of 150 at Div H.Q. "D" Coy working on Southern area. Remainder working on preparations for a camp at MOULINET WOOD & accomodation in TERGNIER	7.P.

Army Form C. 2118.

WAR DIARY
or
INTELLIGENCE SUMMARY.
(Erase heading not required.)

1/4th SUFFOLK REGT

Place	Date	Hour	Summary of Events and Information	Remarks and references to Appendices
ROUEZ CAMP	Feb 21st		"B" Coy at work in Southern area. Remainder working on accommodation in TERGNIER & erection of huts in MOLINET WOOD & in connection with R.E. dump at ROUEZ.	P.
ROUEZ CAMP	Feb 22nd		"D" Coy at work in Southern area. Remainder working at TERGNIER, - MOLINET WOOD & R.E. dump ROUEZ. Lieut BANNERMAN rejoined the battalion for duty. 9.1.9.B	P.
ROUEZ CAMP	Feb 23rd		"B" Coy at work in Southern area. Remainder at TERGNIER, MOLINET WOOD & R.E. dump ROUEZ.	P.
ROUEZ CAMP	Feb 24th		The battalion less A & D. Coy left ROUEZ CAMP at 9.30 A.M & marched to CHAUNY-SUD arriving at 10.45 A.M. Billeted in Southern end of the town. 'A' Coy proceeded to TERGNIER. 'D' Coy continued with their work on Southern area.	P.
CHAUNY	Feb 25th		H.Q + C. Coy left CHAUNY at 10 A.M & moved to BICHADCOURT arriving 10.45. Remainder of day spent improving billets. 'A' + 'D' Coy at work on Divisional area.	P.

WAR DIARY
or
INTELLIGENCE SUMMARY.

(Erase heading not required.)

1/4th SUFFOLK REGT.

Army Form C. 2118.

Vol 29

Place	Date	Hour	Summary of Events and Information	Remarks and references to Appendices
BICHANCOURT	Feb 26th		"A" & "D" Coy at work on Divisional area. "B" & "C" Coy at work on roads & billets at CHAUNY & BICHANCOURT.	I.P.
BICHANCOURT	Feb 27th		"A" Coy working with 503 Coy R.E. on left Brigade area, "B" Coy working with 504 Coy R.E. on Centre Brigade, "D" Coy with 511 Coy R.E. on right Brigade area. "C" Coy working on roads in vicinity of BICHANCOURT.	I.P.
BICHANCOURT	Feb 28th		Work continued on Divisional area. Weather turned dull & some rain fell.	I.P.

L. Grosvenor Lt Col
1/3/18 1/4 Suffolk Regt

Army Form C. 2118.

WAR DIARY
or
INTELLIGENCE SUMMARY. 1/4th SUFFOLK R&t

(Erase heading not required.)

Instructions regarding War Diaries and Intelligence
Summaries are contained in F. S. Regs., Part II.
and the Staff Manual respectively. Title pages
will be prepared in manuscript.

Place	Date	Hour	Summary of Events and Information	Remarks and references to Appendices
BICHANCOURT	Feb 1st		Work on Divisional area. Weather cold.	T.P
BICHANCOURT	Mch 2nd		Work in Divisional area. Weather cold & wet. 2nd Lieut S. EAMAN STILL joined for duty	T.P
BICHANCOURT	Mch 3rd		Work on Divisional area. Weather cold. Snow fell during night	T.P
BICHANCOURT	Mch 4th		Worked in Divisional area. Weather cold with snow cover. In order to organise on the basis of a three company platoon Company 'C' has been broken up & officers + O.R. of this company were distributed amongst A, B, & D Coys. Capt T.W.T SANCTUARY joined for duty	T.P

J. Gifford Lt Col

(A 283) Wt W8.9/M1672 50,000 4/17 Sch 52a Forms/C2118/14 D.D. & L., London, B.C.

Army Form C. 2118.

WAR DIARY
or
INTELLIGENCE SUMMARY. 1/4th SUFFOLK REGT

(Erase heading not required.)

Place	Date	Hour	Summary of Events and Information	Remarks and references to Appendices
BICHANCOURT	Mch 5th		Work on Divisional area.	A.P.
BICHANCOURT	Mch 6th		Work on Divisional area	A.P.
BICHANCOURT	Mch 7th		Work on Divisional area	A.P.
BICHANCOURT	Mch 8th		Work on Divisional area	A.P.
			Capt D.M. French & 2nd Lieut- Bloomfield joined for duty	
BICHANCOURT	Mch 9th		Work on Divisional area.	A.P.
BICHANCOURT	Mch 10th		Work on Divisional area	A.P.
BICHANCOURT	Mch 11th		Work on Divisional area	A.P.
			"B" Coy moved to SINCENY	

Army Form C. 2118.

WAR DIARY
or
INTELLIGENCE SUMMARY. 1/4th SUFFOLK Regt
(Erase heading not required.)

Instructions regarding War Diaries and Intelligence Summaries are contained in F. S. Regs., Part II. and the Staff Manual respectively. Title pages will be prepared in manuscript.

Place	Date	Hour	Summary of Events and Information	Remarks and references to Appendices
BICHANCOURT	Mch 12th		Work on Divisional area Vicinity of "A" Coy billets at TERGNIER was shelled in the afternoon	LR
BICHANCOURT	Mch 13th		Work on Divisional area	LR
BICHANCOURT	Mch 14th		Work on Divisional area	LR
BICHANCOURT	Mch 15th		Work on Divisional area	LR
BICHANCOURT	Mch 16th		Work on Divisional area	LR
BICHANCOURT	Mch 17th		Work on Divisional area	LR
BICHANCOURT	Mch 18th		Work on Divisional area	LR

Army Form C. 2118.

WAR DIARY
or
INTELLIGENCE SUMMARY.   1/4th SUFFOLK REGT
(Erase heading not required.)

Instructions regarding War Diaries and Intelligence Summaries are contained in F. S. Regs., Part II. and the Staff Manual respectively. Title pages will be prepared in manuscript.

Place	Date	Hour	Summary of Events and Information	Remarks and references to Appendices
BICHANCOURT	Mch 19th		Work on Divisional area. Weather turned dull & a good deal of rain during afternoon & night	1P
BICHANCOURT	Mch 20th		"A" & "D" Coy were given a day's rest. "B" Coy worked on cable trench at LA FERTELLE. At 2.30 P.M. orders received preparing for attack & all came into one house notice to be ready to move. At 5.45 P.M. orders received to man battle stations & Coys proceeded to their allotted positions.	1P
BICHANCOURT	Mch 21st		German offensive commenced. "A" Coy attacked 173rd Bde with battle station at QUESSY did considerable execution to the advancing enemy & maintained their position till withdrawn across the canal at M, this coy continued to fight all day & escaped line in rear of the Buffs from QUESSY to VOUREUIL. "B" Coy attached to 175th Bde remained at SINCENY till 5 P.M. & then moved 3 platoons to CONDREN & one platoon to AMIGNY-ROUBY under 123rd / 174th Bde. D "Coy" attached 174th Bde moved to ROND D'ORLEANS	B. ald.

Army Form C. 2118.

WAR DIARY
or
INTELLIGENCE SUMMARY.
(Erase heading not required.)

Instructions regarding War Diaries and Intelligence Summaries are contained in F. S. Regs., Part II. and the Staff Manual respectively. Title pages will be prepared in manuscript.

Place	Date	Hour	Summary of Events and Information	Remarks and references to Appendices
BICHANCOURT	Mch 21st		Battalion H.Q. remained at BICHANCOURT. Casualties Other Ranks Wd 3	
BICHANCOURT	Mch 22nd		Coy remained attached to brigade. "A" Coy took part in fighting on N bank of the OISE & "B" Coy in & around CONDREN	
BICHANCOURT	Mch 23rd		Coys remained with brigade & assisted in the general defence of the sector. Casualties 2/Lt B. Rushman + 2/Lt N. Pitchford Wd, other Ranks Wd. 24 Kd. 3	
BICHANCOURT	Mch 24th		H.Q. left BICHANCOURT & moved to BESME. "A" Coy under 2nd Lieut SMITH rejoined there at 3.30 A.M. 3 Platoons of "B" Coy came out to SINCENY for night. 2/Lt Potter sick Casualties O.R. NIL. Kd. 1.	

J.A. Thomson Lt Col
Commanding Suffolk Regt

WAR DIARY
or
INTELLIGENCE SUMMARY.

(Erase heading not required.)

1/4th SUFFOLK REGT

Army Form C. 2118.

Instructions regarding War Diaries and Intelligence Summaries are contained in F. S. Regs., Part II. and the Staff Manual respectively. Title pages will be prepared in manuscript.

Place	Date	Hour	Summary of Events and Information	Remarks and references to Appendices
BESMÉ	Mch 25th		Ordered to move to PIERREMANDE & left at 11 A.M. arriving 3.40 P.M. & immediately started work on fresh posts & trenches. 3 platoons "B" Coy. went into bivouac at MANICAMP. Casualties Nil.	
PIERREMANDE	Mch 26th		Left at 4 P.M. & proceeded to ST PAUL AUX BOIS arriving 5.30 P.M. New positions were at once reconnoitred & work commenced.	
ST PAUL AUX BOIS	Mch 27th		Worked on new positions all day & garrisoned them at night.	
ST PAUL AUX BOIS	Mch 28th		Work continued on new positions. One platoon of "D" Coy from AMIGNY-ROUY rejoined. Casualties Nil.	

WAR DIARY
INTELLIGENCE SUMMARY.
1/4th SUFFOLK REGT

Army Form C. 21 ?

Place	Date	Hour	Summary of Events and Information	Remarks and references to Appendices
ST PAUL au Bois	Mch 29th		Worked on positions on the canal line. Remaining three platoons of "B" Coy rejoined	
ST PAUL au Bois	Mch 30th		Continued work on canal line	
ST PAUL au Bois	Mch 31st		Continued work on canal line	

Pioneers.
58th Div.

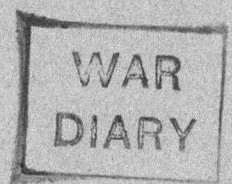

1/4th BATTN. THE SUFFOLK REGIMENT.

A P R I L

1 9 1 8

	At............m.		From............
	To................		
	By...............	(Signature of "Franking Officer.")	By.............

TO	58 DIV		
Sender's Number.	Day of Month.	In reply to Number.	A A A
* DX65	21		

Herewith "War Diary" for "April" 1918.

[signature]

Lt. Col
Comdg. 1/8 Bn Suffolk Regt.

Army Form C. 2118.

INTELLIGENCE SUMMARY
1/4th SUFFOLK REGT
(Erase heading not required.)

98 32

Instructions regarding War Diaries and Intelligence Summaries are contained in F. S. Regs., Part II. and the Staff Manual respectively. Title pages will be prepared in manuscript.

Place	Date	Hour	Summary of Events and Information	Remarks and references to Appendices
ST PAUL AUX BOIS	April 1st		Worked on new line.	
ST PAUL AUX BOIS	April 2nd		Worked on new line.	
ST PAUL AUX BOIS	April 3rd		Relieved by French Bde & moved at 9.30 A.M. by road to LE MESNIL arriving 1.15 P.M. & went into billets. "D" Coy rejoined at 1.30 P.M.	
LE MESNIL	April 4th		Left at 8 A.M. & marched to ST PIERRE-AIGLE arriving 3.30 P.M. & went into billets	
ST PIERRE-AIGLE	April 5th		Remained throughout the day & until 3 A.M.	
ST PIERRE-AIGLE	April 6th		Marched at 3 A.M. to VILLERS-COTTERETS where we entrained & left at 8.20 A.M. for LONGUEAU arriving 1 P.M. After some delay moved at 3.45 P.M. & relieved the 8th Queens Regt in the reserve line at GENTELLES. Relief complete at about 10.15 P.M. Casualties Rd. Other Ranks 1. Wd. — — 1.	

N. Germain

Army Form C. 2118.

WAR DIARY
or
INTELLIGENCE SUMMARY. 1/4th SUFFOLK REGT
(Erase heading not required.)

Instructions regarding War Diaries and Intelligence Summaries are contained in F. S. Regs., Part II. and the Staff Manual respectively. Title pages will be prepared in manuscript.

Place	Date	Hour	Summary of Events and Information	Remarks and references to Appendices
TRENCHES	April 7th		Remained in the line. Work consisted of digging and making huts in the line. Occupied and later connecting up huts and improving accomodation.	
TRENCHES	April 8th		Remained in the line. Weather very wet. Work as usual. H.Qrs. in BOIS DE GENTELLES.	
TRENCHES	April 9th		Remained in the line. A shell fell near to the Billing & made work as usual 6 casualties. Wd. O.R's.	
TRENCHES	April 10th		Remained in line. Work as usual. Capt F.C. CUBITT rejoined from leave & assumed command 1 O.B.O. also Capt T. GASTON R.A.M.C	
Trenches	April 11th		Remained in line. Some shelling of GENTELLES Village on right flank of Dly, another ration mule killed. Work as usual. 6 casualties. W.O. O.R's. 3.	
Trenches	April 12th		Remained on line. Work as usual. 6 casualties Kd. O.R's 1. Wd. O.R's. 1	
Trenches	April 13th		Bn. relieved by 9th Bn London Regt. Relief complete about 8pm. Bn. then remained in the same place and Coys moved to positions	

[signature]

WAR DIARY
or
INTELLIGENCE SUMMARY.

(Erase heading not required.)

Army Form C. 2118.

Instructions regarding War Diaries and Intelligence
Summaries are contained in F. S. Regs., Part II.
and the Staff Manual respectively. Title pages
will be prepared in manuscript.

Place	Date	Hour	Summary of Events and Information	Remarks and references to Appendices
			in the GENTELLES SWITCH between the village and the AMIENS – DOMART Road	
	April 14th		Remained in line working on new position. Lt. H. M. BROWN (31st Div H.Q.) died of wds.	
	April 15th		Remained in line. Coys commenced work on a line of posts near DOMART.	
	April 16th		Remained in line. Work on DOMART line.	
	April 17th		Remained in line. Work on DOMART line.	
	April 18th		Remained in line. Work on DOMART line. Belts at Box's used by 2 Coys.	
	April 19th		Remained in line. Work on DOMART line. Remainder of Bn. in support [?]	

Army Form C. 2118.

WAR DIARY
or
INTELLIGENCE SUMMARY.
(Erase heading not required.)

Instructions regarding War Diaries and Intelligence Summaries are contained in F. S. Regs., Part II. and the Staff Manual respectively. Title pages will be prepared in manuscript.

Place	Date	Hour	Summary of Events and Information	Remarks and references to Appendices
	March 20th		Capt A C HAPPELL took over the duty of 2nd Lieut W ASTILL left the Bn for duty with the RAF	
	March 20th		Remained in bait. Work in Donart Line and cache Bd Fd Dly was detailed to be responsible for "SHEPHERD'S Force" and moved almost to its former position North of FESTUBERT Capt S Gardiner returned from detached duty at BHQ and resumed command of B Bdy	
	April 21st		Remained in bait. Agent BS Cy worked on the HACT Line and Dly the A Ht Switch	
	April 22nd		Remained in bait. March 21"	

J N Grenfell Lt Col Cmdg

WAR DIARY
or
INTELLIGENCE SUMMARY.
(Erase heading not required.)

Army Form C. 2118.

Instructions regarding War Diaries and Intelligence Summaries are contained in F. S. Regs., Part II. and the Staff Manual respectively. Title pages will be prepared in manuscript.

Place	Date	Hour	Summary of Events and Information	Remarks and references to Appendices
	April 23rd		Remained in line. Heavy artillery fire at dawn both sides. Worked on N.T.S. Casualties OR 1 wd.	
	April 24th		Enemy bombardment North of about 5.10 am. Battn were shelled out and moved to a position 500 yds south of the wood. SENTILLES WOOD was shelled heavily afterwards and Albert and they were also shelled up to 9 a.m. Bn was ordered to move into the orders of SHEPHERDS FORCE etc CACHY SWITCH just South of CACHY. B.C. was near the STD end the Blue Line. Casualties OR 1 wd. 6	
	April 25		Bn. held new gun Sullis Casualties OR 1 kill 3 wd Sto (?) (?) North of SENTILLES WOOD Casualties 2nd H.B. No cas wd. OR 2 wd 6	
	April 26		D.Coy. Coy. (?) (?) (?) carrying on the SENTILLES SWITCH Casualties OR Cas. 3	

Army Form C. 2118.

WAR DIARY
or
INTELLIGENCE SUMMARY.
(Erase heading not required.)

Instructions regarding War Diaries and Intelligence Summaries are contained in F. S. Regs., Part II. and the Staff Manual respectively. Title pages will be prepared in manuscript.

Place	Date	Hour	Summary of Events and Information	Remarks and references to Appendices
	April 27		Relieved by the French at about 4.30 am & moved 5 miles to N32. After breakfast at 7.30am. Took remainder 5 CASUN and hot lunches and drew packs. Bn then moved off 5 landed at [illegible] [illegible] out into the AMIENS ASYLUM grounds & the [illegible] [illegible] [illegible] at 1pm. The Cake and ad at 5.45[illegible] and HQ Bn. [illegible] 5 MAISON RULAND [illegible] 5 Rugauler billeted at about 7 pm. [illegible] & [illegible] B RENCOURT	
	April 28		The Bn. [illegible] [illegible] in [illegible] of [illegible] The [illegible] work [illegible] at 6.30 am	
	April 29		Parades as for 28"	
	April 30		Parades as for 28". Coys filled in trenches [illegible] [illegible] [illegible] [illegible]	

"A" Form.
MESSAGES AND SIGNALS.

Prefix... Code... m	Words.	Charge.	This message is on a/c of:	Recd. at ......m
Office of Origin and Service Instructions.		Sent		Date........
	At........m		............Service.	From........
	To........			
	By........		(Signature of "Franking Officer.")	By........

TO	58 Division

Sender's Number.	Day of Month.	In reply to Number.	AAA
SU/235	4		

Herewith War Diary for
May 1918 to be passed to Bde

4th Field Coy
Right OC
Comdg 4 Suffolk Regt

From			
Place			
Time			

The above may be forwarded as now corrected. (Z)

Censor. Signature of Addressor or person authorised to telegraph in his name.
* This line should be erased if not required.

WAR DIARY
or
INTELLIGENCE SUMMARY.
(Erase heading not required.)

1/4 Suffolk

Army Form C. 2118.

Place	Date	Hour	Summary of Events and Information	Remarks and references to Appendices
MAISON ROLLAND	May 1st		Coys carried out ordinary training parades.	
"	2nd		Training parades. Coy pay out.	
"	3rd		Training parades. Range practice	
"	4th		Training parades. Baths and clean clothes for A Coy. Concentration amongst the "Gods" Concert party	
"	5th		Baths and clean clothes for HQ B and D Coys. Church parade at 12 noon. Concert in the evening by the "Q's" (regimental) Concert party	
"	6th		Training parades. The transport moved off at 10 am to BOURDON for MOLIENS AUX BOIS	
"	7th		The Bn. entrained at COULONVILLERS at 9 am and arrived at a wood S.E.	

Commanding 1/4th Suffolk

WAR DIARY
or
INTELLIGENCE SUMMARY.

(Erase heading not required.)

Army Form C. 2118.

Place	Date	Hour	Summary of Events and Information	Remarks and references to Appendices
Wood S.E. of MOLIENS au BOIS	May 8th		Bt MOLIENS au BOIS about 2.30 pm. The Transport arrived about ½ hour before the Bn. There were only about 15 tents for the Bn. The Division became Divisional on Corps Reserve. Bn moved at 1.30 pm to BOIS ROBERT near BAZIEUX taking its Cooks and transport cases on the way. The M.M. was awarded to the following two men at Div. 26544 Pte E. PATTON, 200684 Pte J. H. CHAPLIN, D. Coy. and a Bar to the M.M. to	
BOIS ROBERT		9am	O.C. Coys went to see work to be done at 6am and the Bn went to work at 9am on Trenches in the BAZIEUX System afternoon about 4pm	
		10	60 per Coy worked as for 9am and 60 per Coy did steady shifts working on dug-outs with a time [?] Coy [?] [?] [?] Warned Orders received to move from Brigade. Move however cancelled by Brigade	

WAR DIARY or INTELLIGENCE SUMMARY.

Army Form C. 2118.

(Erase heading not required.)

Instructions regarding War Diaries and Intelligence Summaries are contained in F. S. Regs., Part II. and the Staff Manual respectively. Title pages will be prepared in manuscript.

Place	Date	Hour	Summary of Events and Information	Remarks and references to Appendices
BOIS ROBERT	May 11th		Work as for 10th	
"	12th		Work as for 11th. Evening service at 6.30 pm	
"	13th		Work as for 12th	
"	14th		Work as for 13th	
"	15th		Work as for 14th	
"	16th		Bn moved at 2pm to a camp on V.25.e central near WARLOY taking over from the 1st R.W.F. (having Bn of 47 Div) The London Rifle on the left sector of the Corps front	
"	17th		Bn HQ moved at about 9 pm to n/a of HENENCOURT CHATEAU and Coys	

N. Spencer
Lt Col
L. Suffolk Regt

WAR DIARY or INTELLIGENCE SUMMARY

Army Form C. 2118.

Place	Date	Hour	Summary of Events and Information	Remarks and references to Appendices
Trenches near HEBUTERNE	May 18		to positions in COPSE and COURT trenches just East of HEBUTERNE. After taking over these positions Coy proceeded to work. A and B Coys manning MELBOURNE trench and B Coy digging a new trench. The Bn was to act as reserve Bn and to support Brigade subjected and to form the garrison of COPSE and COURT trenches. B Coy on the Rt, A Coy in the centre and D Coy on the Left. (COPSE support.) C Coy accommodated in a trench just to rear of A Coy and D Coy was on Eoupe on the Chateau grounds near 15,442 to A Coy HQ of 2 platoons in and about Copse Trench & 2 back at "B" Echelon.	
"	"	19th	Work at night as for 17th. Some men employed for burying Self to improve parapets and Little putting in. work as for 18th.	
"	"	20th	Work as for 19th. Casualties 2Lieut A.H.H. SYKES wounded, 1 O.R. killed and 3 wounded all B Coy, by aeroplane bomb.	Lt Colonel Suffolk Regt

WAR DIARY
or
INTELLIGENCE SUMMARY.

Army Form C. 2118.

Place	Date	Hour	Summary of Events and Information	Remarks and references to Appendices
Trenches in HENENCOURT	May 21st		Work as usual, A Coy wiring. B and D Coys digging. [struck through]	
"	22nd		B and D Coys exchanged positions at about 9.15 pm. Left of our front. B Coy came back to Bn HQ. Work as usual. Casualties 2 O.R. wounded at Bn HQ	
"	23rd		Work as usual, half A Coy went Alexander PK digging. Major L.C. ARBUTHNOT joined the Bn for duty.	
"	24th		Bn concerned a new C.T. belonging Australia 57 Westroops. Weather turned wet. B Coy had baths and clean clothes	
"	25th		A and B Coys worked as before. D Coy worked on another C.T. further forward.	
"	26th		A and D Coys worked as the 25th. B Coy had a night off	

Army Form C. 2118.

WAR DIARY
or
INTELLIGENCE SUMMARY.
(Erase heading not required.)

Place	Date	Hour	Summary of Events and Information	Remarks and references to Appendices
Trenches near HENENCOURT	May 27th		D Coy worked as on 26th; B Coy as for A Coy on 26th. A Coy had a night off. A and B Coys exchanged positions at about 9.15 pm	
"	28th		A Coy worked all day on a new Divn HQ. B Coy took over D Coys night work. D Coy had a night off.	
"	29th		D Coy took over A Coys day work at Divn HQ. A Coy took over B Coys night work. A Coy had baths and clean clothes during the morning.	
"	30th		B Coy took over D Coys day work at Divn HQ. A and D Coys worked at night in CAREY ST and MURRAY trench respectively. Casualties. OR. K1.	
"	31st		Bn was relieved by the 8th R Sussex Regt. Relief complete about 10.30 pm. HQ and A Coy moved to a wood just North of KAIZIEUX. B and D Coys moved to BOIS ROBERT. The transport remained as before. Casualties. OR. Wd. 1.	

J. A. Gemmer
Lt Col
4th Suffolk Regt

WAR DIARY
or
INTELLIGENCE SUMMARY
(Erase heading not required.)

Army Form C. 2118.

Place	Date	Hour	Summary of Events and Information	Remarks and references to Appendices
	May 31st		The following Officers were awarded the Military Cross on 3rd May 1918:— Lieut. H. B. HUTCHERSON. The undermentioned N.C.O's & men were awarded the Military Medal on 27th April 1918:— Sgt. C.G. HOTSON 18444 Cpl. G. CLAYDON 20/813 L/Cpl F. J. SAMUELS 19814 Pte. L. TRESHER 20/823 " B. COLLARD 202966 " F. SMITH 235675	

In France
Lieut. Col.
1/4th Suffolk Regt.

Private Confidential

58th Division

Trench War Diary
of the Battalion for
June 1918

[signature]
Major
Comdg 1/4th Suffolk Regt

1/4TH BATTALION,
SUFFOLK
REGIMENT.

Army Form C. 2118.

WAR DIARY
~~INTELLIGENCE SUMMARY.~~
(Erase heading not required.)

1/4th SUFFOLK REGT. Vol 34

Instructions regarding War Diaries and Intelligence Summaries are contained in F.S. Regs., Part II. and the Staff Manual respectively. Title pages will be prepared in manuscript.

Place	Date	Hour	Summary of Events and Information	Remarks and references to Appendices
N. of BAIZIEUX.	JUNE 1st		H.Q. Dudley Y.A. Coy in wood N. of BAIZIEUX 2 Coys & Transport in BOIS ROBERT. Continued work with tunnelling Coy & on the BAIZIEUX system	JP
N. of BAIZIEUX	JUNE 2nd		Work on for 1st line. Played 4th Bn R.W.F.s at football & lost 3-1.	JP
N. of BAIZIEUX	JUNE 3rd		Work with tunnelling Coy & on BAIZIEUX system	JP
N. of BAIZIEUX	JUNE 4th		Work continued. Received orders to be prepared to move	JP
W. of BAIZIEUX	JUNE 5th		Moved at 3. P.M & marched to a bivouac camp in a wood N of BEAUCOURT (DAILY MAIL WOOD) arriving 4.45 P.M. The Division now becomes G.H.Q reserve.	JP
N. of BEAUCOURT	June 6th		Coy inspection	JP

Army Form C. 2118.

WAR DIARY
or
INTELLIGENCE SUMMARY.
(Erase heading not required.)

1/4th SUFFOLK REGT

Place	Date	Hour	Summary of Events and Information	Remarks and references to Appendices
N OF BEAUCOURT	JUNE 7TH		Baths + short parades in morning	F.P.
N OF BEAUCOURT	JUNE 8TH		Parades under Coy commanders in morning. Football + other games in afternoon	F.P.
N OF BEAUCOURT	JUNE 9TH		Church parade 10 A.M.	F.P.
N OF BEAUCOURT	JUNE 10TH		Left camp at 8.45 A.M + marched to a point on the HÉRISSART — PUNCHEVILLERS road arriving 10.10 A.M. Halt, the regiment entrained + left at 12.40 P.M arriving at PICQUIGNY 4.30 P.M. detrained + marched to CROUY arriving 5.50 P.M + going into billets. Transport arrived 8.30 P.M.	F.P.
CROUY	JUNE 11TH		Coy inspections + short parade. Remainder of day spent fixing up billets	F.P.
CROUY	JUNE 12TH		Coy parades in morning games + bathing in afternoon	F.P.

Instructions regarding War Diaries and Intelligence Summaries are contained in F. S. Regs., Part II. and the Staff Manual respectively. Title pages will be prepared in manuscript.

Army Form C. 2118.

WAR DIARY
INTELLIGENCE SUMMARY.
(Erase heading not required.)

Place	Date	Hour	Summary of Events and Information	Remarks and references to Appendices
CROUY	JUNE 13th		Company training in morning. Football, bathing in afternoon. Major General F.W. RAMSAY C.M.G., D.S.O assumed command of the Division.	A.P.
CROUY	JUNE 14th		Company training in morning. Lecture on gas by Divisional Gas Officer in afternoon. Divisional Band played from 4 to 7 P.M. & was much appreciated.	A.P.
CROUY	JUNE 15th		Company training continued	A.P.
CROUY	JUNE 16		Church Parade in the morning. Battalion Transport moved from to MOLIENS AUX BOIS. No a (S.E. of village).	
	JUNE 17		Paraded for entraining at 5 a.m. & started on at 8.30 a.m. Moved to BOIS ROBERT (BAZIEUX) arriving at noon. Moved out to line at 9.30 p.m. taking over from 4th R.M. Fusiliers. H.Q. at AMIENS — ALBERT road south of LAVIEVILLE. A Coy remained on BOIS ROBERT with B Echelon. Transport at Courcelles.	
TRENCHES	JUNE 18th		Work on trenches at night. D Coy working forward on DOG TRENCH B Coy working in rear of Bn. H.Q. on LAVIEVILLE TRENCH improving accommodation etc.	

Army Form C. 2118.

1/1st Bn Suffolk Regt

WAR DIARY
INTELLIGENCE SUMMARY
(Erase heading not required.)

Place	Date	Hour	Summary of Events and Information	Remarks and references to Appendices
TRENCHES	JUNE 19		Work as on 15th June. 1 O.R. wounded D boy	
TRENCHES	JUNE 20		Two Platoons sent to carry a trench on ridge in rear of D by H.Q. (1 O.R. wounded D by) LT J McBARRETT joined for duty.	
TRENCHES	JUNE 21		C.A. boy came up & relieved D by. B by relieved D by (rear) & D by going back to Bois ROBERT. No hours commenced on new trench running North from square later called DITTON TRENCH	
TRENCHES	JUNE 22		Work on DITTON TRENCH	
TRENCHES	JUNE 23		Work on DITTON TRENCH. Battle Surplus reported for duty. LT J. Mc BARRETT & 4 O.R. wounded & B by & 1 O.R. Died of Wounds, B by	
TRENCHES	JUNE 24		Work on DITTON TRENCH (1 O.R. wounded e.g. by)	

Army Form C. 2118.

WAR DIARY
INTELLIGENCE SUMMARY
(Erase heading not required.)

1/4 R. Welsh Fus. Regt.

Place	Date	Hour	Summary of Events and Information	Remarks and references to Appendices
TRENCHES	JUNE 28"		2Lt KELLY C.F. joined for duty. Moth on DITTON TRENCH. Lewis Platoons D Coy moved up from BOIS ROBERT on the night of 28th to join LAVIEVILLE LINE. 1 O.R. wounded. 29th 1 O.R. wounded of B Coy.	
TRENCHES	JUNE 26		Work on DITTON TRENCH D right of LAVIEVILLE LINE. 1,2,3,4 Platoons of D Coy came up from BOIS ROBERT with LAVIEVILLE TRENCH. One Platoon of Coy relieved one Platoon of B Coy in strong point of B.Co. in Bois Robert.	
TRENCHES	JUNE 29"		The Platoons of B Coy moved to Bois Robert after completing night work & from this left a later moving and carrying party and night in BOIS ROBERT with on DUTTON TRENCH D LAVIEVILLE LINE. 2Lts. Q.M. HARTLEY & M.N. NEWBERY joined for duty	
TRENCHES	JAN 28th		Two Coys working on DITTON TRENCH D & C testing	
TRENCHES	JUNE 29"		Two Coys working on DITTON TRENCH. 1 B Coy working on DOG TRENCH	
TRENCHES	JUNE 30		B Coy working on DOG TRENCH & 249. D Coys working near LAVIEVILLE LINE. One OR. wounded. D Coy by enemy bomb.	

J.C. Greenslade Lt Col
1/4 Bn R Welsh Fus

SECRET

> 1/4TH BATTALION,
> SUFFOLK
> REGIMENT.
> No. KA/220
> Date 11-8-18

Headquarters
58th Division

Herewith War Diary
of this Battalion for
July 1918

Pretty Major
for Lieut Col
Comdg 1/4 Suffolk Regt

Army Form C. 2118.

WAR DIARY
or
INTELLIGENCE SUMMARY.   4th SUFFOLK REGT

(Erase heading not required.)

WD 35

Place	Date	Hour	Summary of Events and Information	Remarks and references to Appendices
TRENCHES	JULY 1		2 Coy & D Coy working on new trench running from HIBROW southwards. B Coy resting.	
TRENCHES	JULY 2		B Coy working on DOG TRENCH. C & D Coy & B Coy on new trench.	
TRENCHES	JULY 3		B Coy & C & D Coy working as last day. All D Coy ratty. Revd F.G. Fflloff sick to Hospital.	
TRENCHES	JULY 4		B Coy working on DOG TRENCH & A & D Coy working on new trench.	
TRENCHES	JULY 5		B Coy & D Coy working on new trench. B & D Coy resting. Capt EVERITT came up for duty from B'Echelon. 2/Lieut BOLINGBROKE & 2 Coy rec' bayt PARRY-CROOKE to PRIEUR MANOR.	
TRENCHES	JULY 6		B Coy working on DOG TRENCH. B & D Coy resting on new trench. 2nd Lieut Thistleth'te Platoon working on DOG TRENCH today. 2 or 3 men hit on way home. C.G.R. Little & Rutd Dowson on platoon working on new trench today. Each Platoon loses now & then one rifleman in Copse. or Suffolk Ave.	
TRENCHES	JULY 7		March up to gardens for BOISROBERT.	

Army Form C. 2118.

WAR DIARY
or
INTELLIGENCE SUMMARY.   4ᵀᴴ SUFFOLK REGᵗ
(Erase heading not required.)

Place	Date	Hour	Summary of Events and Information	Remarks and references to Appendices
TRENCHES	JULY 8ᵀᴴ		A & D Coy digging on DARWIN TRENCH, B. Coy on DOG TRENCH	4 P.
TRENCHES	JULY 9ᵀᴴ		A & D Coys digging on DARWIN TRENCH. B Coy worked on DOG TRENCH which is completed. Casualties 1 O.R. Killed 2 O.R. wounded	4 P.
TRENCHES	JULY 10ᵀᴴ		A & B Coys completed the digging of DARWIN TRENCH. 'D' Coy making Lt. Col H.C. COPEMAN went on leave & MAJOR PRETTY assumed command.	4 P.
TRENCHES	JULY 11ᵀᴴ		Wiring of DARWIN TRENCH started, all coys worked on this	4 P.
TRENCHES	JULY 12ᵀᴴ		B & D Coy continued wiring DARWIN TRENCH. 'A' Coy resting	4 P.
TRENCHES	JULY 13ᵀᴴ		'A' Coy had one platoon at work on DARWIN TRENCH & 2 platoons digging completion of DELHI TRENCH. B Coy 2 platoons completed first belt of wire on DARWIN TRENCH & 2 platoons improving DELHI TRENCH. 'D' Coy working on LAVIÉVILLE TRENCH	4 P.

4ᵗʰ Suffolk Regᵗ

Army Form C. 2118.

WAR DIARY
INTELLIGENCE SUMMARY. 4TH SUFFOLK REGT

(Erase heading not required.)

Instructions regarding War Diaries and Intelligence Summaries are contained in F. S. Regs., Part II. and the Staff Manual respectively. Title pages will be prepared in manuscript.

Place	Date	Hour	Summary of Events and Information	Remarks and references to Appendices
TRENCHES	JULY 14TH		A & B Coys manning DARWIN TRENCH. D. Coy digging on DELHI LANE & LAVIÉVILLE TRENCH. 6 O.R. joined the bn for duty	
TRENCHES	JULY 15TH		A Coy digging DELHI LANE. D Coy manning DARWIN TRENCH. B Coy resting	
TRENCHES	JULY 16TH		A Coy digging LAVIÉVILLE TRENCH, B & D completed the manning of DARWIN TRENCH	
TRENCHES	JULY 17TH		A & B Coys digging LAVIÉVILLE TRENCH & DURBAN TRENCH. D Coy resting	
TRENCHES	JULY 18TH		A & B Coys manning SHRINE TRENCH. Work interfered with by shelling. D Coy manning LAVIÉVILLE TRENCH. Casualties 2nd Lieut G.P. HARTLEY wounded. 1 O.R killed & 7 O.R wounded. Capt H LEEMING joined the bn.	
TRENCHES	JULY 19TH		"A" Coy resting. "B" Coy manning SHRINE TRENCH & HILL ROW. D Coy manning LAVIÉVILLE TRENCH. At 1.30 A.M. two bombs were dropped on Bn. Hd. Qrs. Casualties 1 O.R killed	

In Command
4 Suffolk Regt

Army Form C. 2118.

WAR DIARY
or
INTELLIGENCE SUMMARY. 4th SUFFOLK REGT

(Erase heading not required.)

Instructions regarding War Diaries and Intelligence Summaries are contained in F. S. Regs., Part II. and the Staff Manual respectively. Title pages will be prepared in manuscript.

Place	Date	Hour	Summary of Events and Information	Remarks and references to Appendices
TRENCHES	JULY 20TH		"A" Coy digging extension of LAVIÉVILLE TRENCH. "B" Coy dug DERBY LANE. "D" Coy forming LAVIÉVILLE. Casualties 1 O.R. wounded	4P
TRENCHES	JULY 21ST		"A" Coy digging extension to LAVIÉVILLE. "B" Coy worked on its battle position. "D" Coy winning LAVIÉVILLE	4P
TRENCHES	JULY 22ND		"A" Coy winning on S. side of ALBERT ROAD. "D" Coy winning side of trench between PIONEER TRENCH & DERWENT TRENCH. "B" Coy digging. Casualties 1 O.R. wounded	4P
TRENCHES	JULY 23RD		"A" Coy commenced work on approach of mine S. of ALBERT RD & communication trench to DARWIN TRENCH from E. "B" "D" continued winning trench between PIONEER & DERWENT TRENCHES. Weather fine and dry	4P
TRENCHES	JULY 24TH		"A" Coy worked on its battle position. "B" Coy worked on mine S. of ALBERT RD. "D" Coy continued winning trench between PIONEER & water. Casualties 1 O.R. killed 1 O.R. wounded	4P
TRENCHES	JULY 25TH		"A" Coy continued mine S. of ALBERT RD. "B" Coy winning trench between PIONEER & DERWENT TRENCHES. "D" Coy commenced work on a mass of wire between DERWENT & DARWIN TRENCHES winning approach to DARWIN TRENCH from S. 2nd Lieut S.L.A. MASTIN rejoined the Bn from R.A.F.	4P

Army Form C. 2118.

WAR DIARY
or
INTELLIGENCE SUMMARY. 4th SUFFOLK REGT
(Erase heading not required.)

Instructions regarding War Diaries and Intelligence Summaries are contained in F. S. Regs., Part II. and the Staff Manual respectively. Title pages will be prepared in manuscript.

Place	Date	Hour	Summary of Events and Information	Remarks and references to Appendices
TRENCHES	JULY 26TH		"A" Coy rested. "B" Coy on N. maze & mine. D' on S. mine & mine. Lt Col H.C. COPEMAN C.M.G. D.S.O returned from leave & resumed command of the Bn.	4R
TRENCHES	JULY 27TH		"A" & "B" Coys at work on N. maze & mine. D' Coy on S. maze	4R
TRENCHES	JULY 28TH		"A" & "B" Coys worked on N. maze & mine. D' Coy on S. maze. Lt HOYLAND joined for duty, from 6 months in England	4R
TRENCHES	JULY 29TH		A Coy worked on N. maze. B Coy rested. D Coy worked on LAVIEVILLE Trench.	
-	-	30th	A Coy worked on N. maze; B and D Coys in LAVIEVILLE Trench	
-	-	31st	As for 30th. Two bombs were dropped near Bn HQrs. Except this by Enemy.	

J.R. Grenier Lt Col
4 Suffolk Regt

58th Divl. Troops

4th BATTALION

SUFFOLK REGIMENT (PIONEERS)

AUGUST 1918

Army Form C. 2118.

WAR DIARY
or
INTELLIGENCE SUMMARY.   4th SUFFOLK REGT

(Erase heading not required.)

Instructions regarding War Diaries and Intelligence
Summaries are contained in F. S. Regs., Part II.
and the Staff Manual respectively. Title pages
will be prepared in manuscript.

Place	Date	Hour	Summary of Events and Information	Remarks and references to Appendices
TRENCHES.	Aug 1st		Work continued on LAVIÉVILLE TRENCH & the ALBERT ROAD	J.P.
TRENCHES.	Aug 2nd		Left trenches at 11.45 P.M & marched to BOIS ROBERT arriving about 2.15 A.M. & encamped for the remainder of the night.	J.P.
BOIS ROBERT	Aug 3rd		Left BOIS ROBERT at 2.45 P.M & marched to BEHENCOURT where the regiment entrained & started at 5 P.M for VILLERS BOCAGE arriving 7.10 P.M & going into billets. Weather turned wet.	J.P.
VILLERS BOCAGE	Aug 4th		Rested. Very wet day. Capt & 2. M.H.R. HARRISON joined the battalion	J.P.
VILLERS BOCAGE	Aug 5th		Entrained at 10 P.M & proceeded to LAHOUSSOYE arriving 1.30 A.M. Returned & marched to BOIS ESCARDONNEUSE where we camped for the remainder of the night. 2 officers & 50. O.R. went to BONNAY for work on R.E. dump.	J.P.

WAR DIARY
or
INTELLIGENCE SUMMARY. 4TH SUFFOLK REGT

(Erase heading not required.)

Army Form C. 2118.

Place	Date	Hour	Summary of Events and Information	Remarks and references to Appendices
BOIS ESCARDONNEUSE	Aug 6th		Remained in the wood & spent day erecting bivouacs & shelter. A few shells fell in transport lines. Casualties 1 O.R. wounded.	J.P.
BOIS ESCARDONNEUSE	Aug 7th		Battalion moved forward to dug-outs in a gully N.W. of SAILLY-LE-SEC starting 9.15 P.M. & arriving 12 midnight. 3 Platoons of "A" Coy & 3 of "D" Coy were detailed for various consolidation duties with regiments of 173rd Bde. "B" Coy & 1 platoon "A" Coy remained at Bn H.Q.	J.P.
TRENCHES	Aug 8th		58th Division took part in general attack by 4th Army which commenced at 4.20 A.M. At 10 A.M. orders were received for "B" Coy & 1 Plt "A" Coy to go forward & dig line of posts protecting left flank of Divisional front where the remainder of the Bn were already working. Bn H.Q. moved forward to valley N of SAILLY LAURETTE Casualties 9 O.R. killed 20 O.R. wounded.	J.P.
N of SAILLY LAURETTE	Aug 9th		Working parties withdrawn at 2. P.M preparation to push attack to be launched at 5.30 P.M. At midnight the battalion again went forward & dug a line of posts between CORBIE – BRAY road & GRESSAIRE WOOD on new front line, getting back to bivouacs at 5 A.M. Casualties 1 O.R. wounded.	J.P.

The Officer commanding
4th Suffolk Regt
Lieut Col

Army Form C. 2118.

WAR DIARY
or
INTELLIGENCE SUMMARY. 4th SUFFOLK REGt

(Erase heading not required.)

Instructions regarding War Diaries and Intelligence Summaries are contained in F. S. Regs., Part II. and the Staff Manual respectively. Title pages will be prepared in manuscript.

Place	Date	Hour	Summary of Events and Information	Remarks and references to Appendices
N of SAILLY LAURETTE	Aug 10th		Returned to BOIS ESCARDONNEUSE starting at 5.30 P.M. & arriving 8.30 P.M.	F.P
BOIS ESCARDONNEUSE	Aug 11th		Rested during the day. At 4 P.M received orders to go forward again. Marched at 5 P.M & reached a point N of SAILLY LAURETTE cemetery at 8.15 P.M where Bn H.Q. were established & the Bn rested till 9.30 P.M. One Company was then detailed to work with each Coys of R.E's. The work consisted of carrying wire etc to be placed in parts of trench dug previous night. In the valley were pull of gas believed to be caused by explosion of dump of gas shells. Work could not be done & battalion returned to Bn H.Q. all being back by 5.30 A.M.	F.P
N of SAILLY LAURETTE	Aug 12th		Rested during the day & moved at 8.30 P.M to complete the work of previous night. This was successfully accomplished & parties back at Bn H.Q. by 4.45 A.M. H.M. The King interviewed representatives from all units of the Div. Two O.R from the Bn went to QUERRIEU for this parade	F.P

Lt Colonel 4th Suffolk Regt

Army Form C. 2118.

WAR DIARY
or
INTELLIGENCE SUMMARY.   4TH SUFFOLK REGT
(Erase heading not required.)

Instructions regarding War Diaries and Intelligence Summaries are contained in F. S. Regs., Part II. and the Staff Manual respectively. Title pages will be prepared in manuscript.

Place	Date	Hour	Summary of Events and Information	Remarks and references to Appendices
N of SAILLY LAURETTE	Aug 13th		Moved at 2.30 P.M to return to Bois ESCARDONNEUSE. On the way the regiment bathed in the SOMME & reached bivouacs in the wood 7.30 P.M	4P
Bois ESCARDONNEUSE	Aug 14th		Day spent making camp & cleaning up	4P
Bois ESCARDONNEUSE	Aug 15th		Coy inspections & one hour drill	4P
Bois ESCARDONNEUSE	Aug 16th		Coy parades from 9 to 12.45. 1 Platoon of "B" Coy detached to MORLANCOURT for salvage work	4P
Bois ESCARDONNEUSE	Aug 17th		Coy parades from 9 to 12. Bn parade from 12.15 to 12-45. Games in afternoon	4P
Bois ESCARDONNEUSE	Aug 18th		Church parade at 10.30.	4P
Bois ESCARDONNEUSE	Aug 19th		Training continued Inter-half-Coy football competition commenced	4P

L. P. Greeve Lieut. Col.
Comdg. 4 Suffolk Regt.

Army Form C. 2118.

WAR DIARY
or
INTELLIGENCE SUMMARY. 4TH SUFFOLK REGT
(Erase heading not required.)

Instructions regarding War Diaries and Intelligence Summaries are contained in F. S. Regs., Part II. and the Staff Manual respectively. Title pages will be prepared in manuscript.

Place	Date	Hour	Summary of Events and Information	Remarks and references to Appendices
Bois EscARDONNEUSE	Aug 20th		Training continued. Major General F.W. Ramsay C.M.G. D.S.O. Commanding 58TH Division inspected the battalion at training.	
			Foot-ball competition continued.	F.P.
			Capt. T.S. Cubitt left on appointment as 2nd in Command to 12TH Bn London Regt	
Bois EscARDONNEUSE	Aug 21st		Training continued.	
			A battalion whist-drive was held in the afternoon with 304 entries. Proceeds amounting to 720 francs were sent in aid of Suffolks P.O.W. fund.	F.P.
			The "Gooch" concert party gave a performance at 5.30 P.M.	
			2nd Lt. W. Berwick joined the battalion for duty	
Bois EscARDONNEUSE	Aug 22nd		Training continued.	
			Football & cricket in afternoon	F.P.
Bois EscARDONNEUSE	Aug 23rd		Training continued	
			Football & cricket matches in afternoon	F.P.

L.M. Youngman Lieut Col
Commdg 4th Suffolk Regt

Army Form C. 2118.

WAR DIARY
or
INTELLIGENCE SUMMARY.   4TH SUFFOLK REGT

(Erase heading not required.)

Place	Date	Hour	Summary of Events and Information	Remarks and references to Appendices
BOIS ESCARDONNEUSE	Aug 24th		Moved at 6 A.M. & marched to gully S. of MERICOURT arriving 7.40 A.M & spent day making bivouacs. During day orders were received to move again & we left at 9 P.M. & proceeded to some trenches about half a mile W. of BOIS de TAILLES & N. of CORBIE—BRAY road arriving 11 P.M. Two platoons detailed for special work with R.E. Battle surplus remained at BOIS ESCARDONNEUSE	JP
WEST OF BOIS de TAILLES	Aug 25th		58th Division attacked at 2.30 A.M but the regt was not called upon to take part & was employed in repairing roads. The battle surplus of 7 O.O.R. reported to A.D.S. for work as stretcher bearers in event of them being required. Transport moved forward to valley in BOIS de TAILLES. N. of CORBIE—BRAY road. Heavy thunderstorm	JP
WEST OF BOIS de TAILLES	Aug 26th		Continued work on roads. Some rain	JP

Army Form C. 2118.

WAR DIARY
or
INTELLIGENCE SUMMARY. 4TH SUFFOLK REGT

(Erase heading not required.)

Instructions regarding War Diaries and Intelligence Summaries are contained in F. S. Regs., Part II. and the Staff Manual respectively. Title pages will be prepared in manuscript.

Place	Date	Hour	Summary of Events and Information	Remarks and references to Appendices
WEST OF BOIS DU TAILLES	AUG 27TH		58th Division attached at 4.55 A.M. We continued watching on outposts & outlying. 2nd Lt A.J. ALDOUS joined the battalion for duty	JR
WEST of BOIS du TAILLES	AUG 28th		Marched at 10.30 A.M. & proceed to valley N.E. of BRAY arriving 12 noon. Moved again at 8 P.M. & relieved the 2/2nd London Regt on left of divisional front in BOIS d'en HAUT E. of MARICOURT. Relief complete 3.35 A.M. 4 O.R. joined for duty.	JR
BOIS D'EN HAUT	AUG 29th		"B" Coy advanced at 2 P.M. to occupy a trench running S. from MAUREPAS. "A" coy went forward at 3.30 P.M. Passed through "B" Coy position & occupied a trench about 800 yds in advance of it. Bn. Hdqrs 2nd & "D" Coy were the minute unchanged to position S. of MAUREPAS & "B" Coy joined "A" Coy. 2nd Lt A.H. ALLATT joined bn for duty	JR

M. Anderson Lieut Col
Comdg 4th Suffolk Regt

WAR DIARY
or
INTELLIGENCE SUMMARY.   4TH SUFFOLK REGT

Army Form C. 2118.

Place	Date	Hour	Summary of Events and Information	Remarks and references to Appendices
S of MAUREPAS.	Aug 30th		175 Bde own ghened moved forward at 5.A.M & "A" Coy sent forward two platoons to get touch with them at 9.30 A.M. Battalion advanced at 12 noon with 10TH Londons Regt on its right to ridge running S from HOSPITAL FARM. HILL 150. Shelling fairly heavy during the day. Having reached our position 9th Bn London Regt passed through us to mop up MARRIÈRES WOOD. Casualties 2 O.R. killed 10. O.R. wounded. Capt C.P. Perry-Crooke & 2nd Lieut H.T.E. Oakerly slightly wounded remained at duty.	F. F.
S of HOSPITAL WOOD	Aug 31st		At dawn 174 Bde passed through our position to attack & at 1.15 P.M we were withdrawn to a trench line 1,500 yds in rear. At 8.20 P.M we moved to S. of MARICOURT arriving 11.30 P.M & camped for night. Casualties 2 O.R. killed & 4 O.R. wounded.	F.

M. Youngman Lieut Col
Comdg 4th Suffolk Regt

WAR DIARY
or
INTELLIGENCE SUMMARY. 4th SUFFOLK REGT

Army Form C. 2118.

(Erase heading not required.)

Place	Date	Hour	Summary of Events and Information	Remarks and references to Appendices
S OF MARICOURT	Sept 1st		Day spent marking bivouacs & shelters. In afternoon we were warned to ready to go forward at ½ hours notice but this was cancelled at 5 P.M.	J.P.
S. OF MARICOURT	Sept 2nd		Cleaning up & making bivouacs. Divisional commander called in morning & congratulated the C.O. on work done by regiment. In the afternoon at a meeting of C.O's the Corps Commander (Lt General Sir A.J. Godley K.C.B., K.C.M.G.) expressed himself as very pleased with the good work done by the Bns during the advance	J.P.
S OF MARICOURT	Sept 3rd		Coy training & every man bathed in the SOMME	J.P.
S OF MARICOURT	Sept 4th		Coy training in morning.	
S OF MARICOURT	Sept 5th		Coy training in morning. Heavy rain & thunderstorm in evening	J.P.

J.C. Cooper
Lieut Col.
Comdg. 4th Batt. Suff. Regt.

Army Form C. 2118.

WAR DIARY
or
INTELLIGENCE SUMMARY.   4TH SUFFOLK REGT

(Erase heading not required.)

Instructions regarding War Diaries and Intelligence Summaries are contained in F. S. Regs., Part II. and the Staff Manual respectively. Title pages will be prepared in manuscript.

Place	Date	Hour	Summary of Events and Information	Remarks and references to Appendices
S OF MARICOURT	SEPT 6TH		Embussed at 5 P.M & proceeded to RANCOURT arriving at 9 P.M spending the night in the open. Transport moved to BOUCHAVESNES to relieve 4/2 R.W.F.	7P
RANCOURT	SEPT 7TH		Mvd at 1 P.M proceeded to a camp E of MOISLAINS arriving 3 P.M Transport joined in here.	7P
E OF MOISLAINS	SEPT 8TH		Mvd at 10 A.M & marched to a camp S of NURLU arriving 11.30.A.M. Remainder of day spent in repairing camp.	7P
S OF NURLU	SEPT 9TH		Worked on roads & salvage. Weather turned very wet.	7P
S OF NURLU	SEPT 10TH		Relieved elements Bn of 3rd, 6th & 7th Battalion London Regt in trenches S & S.W of EPEHY. Left camp at 7.45 P.M & completed relief at 3.30.A.M During the night bombs were dropped on the transport lines causing the following casualties. Capt D.M.FRENCH & 1st O.M.W.BERWICK killed. Capt L.J.RICHARDS & Rev F.G.ALLSOPP & 4.O.R wounded. 42 horses or mules killed & 16 wounded.	7P

W.L. Elwes Capt & Adjt
Comdg 4th Suffolk Regt

Army Form C. 2118.

WAR DIARY
or
INTELLIGENCE SUMMARY. 4TH SUFFOLK REGT

(Erase heading not required.)

Instructions regarding War Diaries and Intelligence Summaries are contained in F.S. Regs., Part II. and the Staff Manual respectively. Title pages will be prepared in manuscript.

Place	Date	Hour	Summary of Events and Information	Remarks and references to Appendices
TRENCHES	Sept 11th		Worked on trenches & front parallel. Relieved by 10th Bn London Regt. Relief commenced 8.30 P.M. & was complete about 3 A.M. All back in camp S. of NURLU by 7.30 A.M. Lt Col H.C. Copeman proceeded on leave & Major F. Pretty assumed command. Casualties 2 O.R. wounded	JP
S. of NURLU	Sept 12th		Day spent cleaning up. Orders received in afternoon for work in front line. Companies left camp at 7 P.M. & returned about 4.30 A.M. Very wet night.	JP
S. of NURLU	Sept 13th		Rested & worked on protection of huts in camp	JP
S. of NURLU	Sept 14th		Orders received to take over front line West of PEIZIERE. Left camp at 7.30 P.M. & relieved the 12th London Regt on left of Divisional boundary. "D" on right of line "B" on left "A" in support. Relief complete 11.45 P.M. Except for a little privileged shelling a quiet night.	JP

Candy H.C. Mother Regt
N.R. Clemence Lieut Col
Comdg 4th Suffolk Regt.

WAR DIARY
or
INTELLIGENCE SUMMARY. 4TH SUFFOLK REGT

(Erase heading not required.)

Army Form C. 2118.

Instructions regarding War Diaries and Intelligence Summaries are contained in F. S. Regs., Part II. and the Staff Manual respectively. Title pages will be prepared in manuscript.

Place	Date	Hour	Summary of Events and Information	Remarks and references to Appendices
TRENCHES.	Sept 15th		Trenches deepened & otherwise improved. Patrols out all night but nothing of importance occurred. Trenches lightly shelled at intervals	YR.
TRENCHES.	Sept 16th		Relieved by 2/4th London Regt. Relief commenced 9.30 P.M & was complete by 11.30. All back in camp by 2.30 A.M. Heavy thunder-storm during the night	YR.
S of NURLU	Sept 17th		Cleaning up & Coy inspections. Work done on camp prutition	YR
S of NURLU	Sept 18th		At 5.15 P.M. orders received to move forward into the line. Regiment paraded & was ready to move at 5.50 P.M when the orders were cancelled & we remained in camp on 1 hour notice	YR
S of NURLU	Sept 19th		Remained in camp ready to go forward at short notice. At 6.30 P.M however a message was received that we should not be required. Reinforcements arrived to replace those lost by bombs.	YR.

Comdg 4th Suffolk Regt.

Army Form C. 2118.

WAR DIARY
or
INTELLIGENCE SUMMARY.   4TH SUFFOLK REGT

(Erase heading not required.)

Instructions regarding War Diaries and Intelligence
Summaries are contained in F. S. Regs., Part II.
and the Staff Manual respectively. Title pages
will be prepared in manuscript.

Place	Date	Hour	Summary of Events and Information	Remarks and references to Appendices
S of NURLU	Sept 20th		Received orders to relieve the 2/2nd London Regt in support trenches East of PEIZIERE. Left camp 6.30 P.M., relief complete 11.35 P.M.	I.R
TRENCHES	Sept 21st		Lt. Col Copeman C.M.G. D.S.O returned from leave & assumed command. Orders were received to be ready to attack & jumping off time tentatively, but attack was postponed.	I.R
TRENCHES	Sept 22nd		In evening A & D Coys moved forward into POPLAR TRENCH & B Coy moved forward by ROOM TRENCH & OCKENDON & took part in an attack on KILDARE POST, DADOS LANE etc attached to 9th Bn London Regt. The attack was successful. "B" Coy took 10 ff & 5 O.R prisoners & captured 2 M.G. Casualties 1 O.R killed, 2nd Lieut B. WEBB & 2 2 O.R wounded.	I.R
TRENCHES	Sept 23rd		"B" Coy remained in front line in sunken road S of KILDARE POST until relieved by a Coy of 9th R.F. in the evening. A & D Coys relieved by 5th Berkshire Regt. IR on relief battalion moved to near VILLERS FAUCON at 3 A.M. & entered at 6 A.M. 24th	I.R

M. Copeman
Comdg 4 Suffolk Regt

Army Form C. 2118.

WAR DIARY
or
INTELLIGENCE SUMMARY. 4TH SUFFOLK REGT.

(Erase heading not required.)

Instructions regarding War Diaries and Intelligence Summaries are contained in F. S. Regs., Part II. and the Staff Manual respectively. Title pages will be prepared in manuscript.

Place	Date	Hour	Summary of Events and Information	Remarks and references to Appendices
BRICQUETERIE CAMP	Sept 24th		Having entrained at 6 A.M proceeded to Bricqueterie Camp, S. of Montauban arriving 9.30 A.M.	F.P
BRICQUETERIE CAMP	Sept 25th		Cleaning up + Coy inspection. Officers visited various localities where the regiment were engaged in the Somme offensive of 1916	F.P
BRICQUETERIE CAMP	Sept 26th		Party of 5 officers + 150 O.R. left camp 3 A.M + marched to Edgehill Station where they entrained all units of 115th brigade group. Transport left at 10 A.M for Edgehill + entrained + remainder of the regiment at 12 P.M	F.P
TRAIN	Sept 27th		Left Edgehill Station 6.40 A.M + travelled via Amiens + St Pol to Aubigny arriving 10 P.M. after some delay we detrained + entrained for a camp S. of Hersin arriving 3 A.M. Transport arrived + remained in Hersin Sep 6.30 A.M. 28th - inst	F.P

(A800) D. D. & L., London, E.C. Wt. W1771/M2031 750,000 5/17 Sch. 92 Forms/C2118/14

In the Capt. Const. 4th Suffolk Regt.

Army Form C. 2118.

WAR DIARY
or
INTELLIGENCE SUMMARY. 4TH SUFFOLK REGT

(Erase heading not required.)

Instructions regarding War Diaries and Intelligence Summaries are contained in F. S. Regs., Part II. and the Staff Manual respectively. Title pages will be prepared in manuscript.

Place	Date	Hour	Summary of Events and Information	Remarks and references to Appendices
CAMP S OF HERSIN	Sept 28th		Remained in camp.	F.
S of HERSIN	Sept 29th		Moved at 11 A.M. & relieved the 12th Notts + Derbys at North Maroc E of Grenay. Grenay. Relief complete 1 P.M. Good accommodation in cellars. Transport moved to GAGNAM BULLY GRÉNAY Very wet night.	F.
MAROC	Sept 30th		2 O.R attached to 503 Coy R.E for railway maintenance. 11 O.R. for work on R.E. dump. 1 off + 26 O.R. for work on divisional farm. 1 O.R wounded & held at redoubt	F.

58

Army Form C. 2118.

WAR DIARY
or
INTELLIGENCE SUMMARY. 4TH SUFFOLK REGT

(Erase heading not required.)

Place	Date	Hour	Summary of Events and Information	Remarks and references to Appendices
MAROC	Oct 1st		Refitting & improvement of accommodation. Lt. E.H. ENRAGHT joined the battalion for duty from hospital	7R
MAROC	Oct 2nd		Day spent on improvement & accommodation & repair of roads in MAROC. 2nd Lt W.D. GRAHAM joined the battalion for duty	7R
MAROC	Oct 3rd		Received orders to move & left MAROC at 5.45 P.M & proceeded to CITÉ ST PIERRE arriving 6.50 P.M. Accommodation in cellars. "D" Coy proceeded at 10.15 P.M for work in forward area returning 4 A.M. 2nd Lieuts G.A. HARGREAVES & S.E. MAHON joined the battalion for duty.	7R
CITÉ ST PIERRE	Oct 4th		"B" Coy left at 5.30 A.M. "A" Coy left at 7.30 A.M for similar work. "B" Coy returned to camp 10.30 A.M & went out again from 5 P.M to 9 P.M. "A" Coy returned at 4.30 P.M. "D" Coy left camp at 8.30 A.M returned 4 P.M. All tasks consisted of making trenches	7R
CITÉ ST PIERRE	Oct 5th		All Coys at work on trenches during day	7R

L.E. Cumming Lt Col
4 Suffolk Regt

58th Division

Herewith War Diary
of this Battalion
for October 1918

[signature]
Lieut-Col
Comdg. 4th Suffolk Regt.

4TH BATTALION,
SUFFOLK
REGIMENT.
No. KA 339
D... 8.11.18

Army Form C. 2118.

WAR DIARY
or
INTELLIGENCE SUMMARY. 4TH SUFFOLK REGT

(Erase heading not required.)

Place	Date	Hour	Summary of Events and Information	Remarks and references to Appendices
CITÉ ST PIERRE	Oct 6th		One company attached to each of the three field Companies R.E. Work consisted mainly of making & repairing trenches forward.	JP
CITÉ ST PIERRE	Oct 7th		Work on trenches.	JP
CITÉ ST PIERRE	Oct 8th		Work on roads, trenches & bridges.	JP
CITÉ ST PIERRE	Oct 9th		Work on roads & trenches.	JP
CITÉ ST PIERRE	Oct 10th		Work on roads & trenches. 2nd Lieuts J.S. ODMAN, J.H. HOWES, J. COE & F.C. ROSE joined for duty	JP

Army Form C. 2118.

WAR DIARY
or
INTELLIGENCE SUMMARY. 4TH SUFFOLK REGT

(Erase heading not required.)

Instructions regarding War Diaries and Intelligence Summaries are contained in F. S. Regs., Part II. and the Staff Manual respectively. Title pages will be prepared in manuscript.

Place	Date	Hour	Summary of Events and Information	Remarks and references to Appendices
CITÉ ST PIERRE	Oct 11th		Work on for previous day	JP
CITÉ ST PIERRE	Oct 12th		Work continued. 2nd Lt G.A. HAYWARD + 2nd Lieut F. ADAMS rejoined for duty. Casualties 2. O.R. wounded.	JP
CITÉ ST PIERRE	Oct 13th		Work continued	JP
CITÉ ST PIERRE	Oct 14th		Work continued. Orders received to move forward tomorrow. Military Medals awarded to Sergt T. LOCKSMITH + Pte W. BARBER + bar to M.M. awarded to Pte W.J. LEGG Stt. M.M. for 2nd time on Sept 10th. with connected harrying of transport.	JP
CITÉ ST PIERRE	Oct 15th		Work continued + on completion battalion proceeded to HARNES. Transport moved up to CITÉ ST PIERRE. Lieut J.C. RASH rejoined for duty. Casualty 1. O.R. wounded	JP

L. Cpl. [signature]
2nd Batt. [signature]

D. D. & L., London, E.C.
(A802) Wt. W1771/M2032 5/17 Sch. 82 Forms/C2118/14

Army Form C. 2118.

WAR DIARY
or
INTELLIGENCE SUMMARY. 4th SUFFOLK REGT

(Erase heading not required.)

Instructions regarding War Diaries and Intelligence
Summaries are contained in F. S. Regs, Part II
and the Staff Manual respectively. Title pages
will be prepared in manuscript.

Place	Date	Hour	Summary of Events and Information	Remarks and references to Appendices
HARNES	Oct 16th		Worked on repair of roads. Military medal awarded to Cpl P. HALL. M.M. & Military medal awarded to Sergt W. E. SMITH & B. MANSFIELD for good work done by them in the attack on KILDARE POST on Sept 22nd.	
HARNES	Oct 17th		Left HARNES at 1.0 P.M. & proceeded to COURRIERS arriving 3.0 P.M. Companies at once forwarded for work on roads & bridges.	
COURRIERS	Oct 18th		Work continued & on completion companies marched to OSTRICOURT & went into billets.	
OSTRICOURT	Oct 19th		Worked on repair of roads & on completion companies marched to MONS EN PÉVÈLE & went into billets.	
MONS en PÉVÈLE	Oct 20th		Left at 9.30 A.M. & marched to AUCHY arriving 11.30 A.M. Companies immediately started work on road repairs, filling in mine craters & temporary bridging	

Army Form C. 2118.

WAR DIARY
or
INTELLIGENCE SUMMARY. 4th SUFFOLK REGT
(Erase heading not required.)

Instructions regarding War Diaries and Intelligence Summaries are contained in F. S. Regs., Part II. and the Staff Manual respectively. Title pages will be prepared in manuscript.

Place	Date	Hour	Summary of Events and Information	Remarks and references to Appendices
AUCHY	Oct. 21st		Work continued as previous day	AP
AUCHY	Oct. 22nd		Work continued. Bn H.Q. & "B" Coy moved to Aix. A & D Coy remained the night in AUCHY.	AP
AIX	Oct. 23rd		"A" Coy moved forward & worked on roads in HOWARDRIES & Bois de RONGY returning to billets in Aix on completion. "B" Coy engaged in making frames in Bois de RONGY & moved into billets at LESDAIN A/N. "D" Coy worked on roads and billeted in HAUT HAMEAU	AP
AIX	Oct. 24th		"A" & "B" Coy making frames. "D" Coy working on roads & bridges.	AP
AIX	Oct. 25th		Work continued as yesterday	AP
Aix	Oct. 26th		H.Q. & "D" Coy moved to billets in RONGY	

D. D. & L., London, E.C.
(A809) W. W1272(M2091 750,000 5/17 Sch. 52. Forms/C2-1/64/4

Army Form C. 2118.

WAR DIARY
or
INTELLIGENCE SUMMARY.   4TH SUFFOLK REGT

(Erase heading not required.)

Instructions regarding War Diaries and Intelligence Summaries are contained in F.S. Regs., Part II. and the Staff Manual respectively. Title pages will be prepared in manuscript.

Place	Date	Hour	Summary of Events and Information	Remarks and references to Appendices
RONGY	Oct 27th		Companies attached to Field Coy. R.E. for work. "A" Coy moved into billets at PLANARD	F.
RONGY	Oct 28th		Worked under direction of Field Coy. Village shelled during night. "A" Coy moved into billets at RONGY. Casualties 2 O.R. wounded.	F.
RONGY	Oct 29th		Work continued under direction of Field Coy. Village again shelled during the night. Casualties 2 O.R. killed 5 O.R. wounded	F.
RONGY	Oct 30th		"D" moved into billets in BELZAMOIS + RUMEGIES. Work continued in conjunction with R.E.	F.
RONGY	Oct 31st		Work continued on yesterday.	F.

58th Division "A".
================

Herewith Original War Diary for the month of November, 1918, for the Battalion under my Command.

December 2nd, 1918.

Lieut-Colonel,
Commanding 58th Battalion, M.G.Corps.

WAR DIARY
or
INTELLIGENCE SUMMARY.

4th SUFFOLK R<u>egt</u>

Army Form C. 2118.

Place	Date	Hour	Summary of Events and Information	Remarks and references to Appendices
RONGY	Nov 1st		Work continued in conjunction with R.E.	JP
RONGY	Nov 2nd		Work continued, consisting chiefly of carrying up rafts, frames & material for bridging the ESCAUT River	JP
RONGY	Nov 3rd		Work continued. Lieut R.A. HAYWARD wounded whilst in working party. 1 O.R. joined the battalion.	JP
RONGY	Nov 4th		Work continued. RONGY & LESDAIN shelled during the night.	JP
RONGY	Nov 5th		Work continued. Considerable shelling throughout the day & night. To the great regret of all ranks Capt J. GASTON M.C. R.A.M.C. was severely wounded & died at the A.D.S. RUMEGIES in the evening. Casualties: Capt J Gaston M.C. R.A.M.C. killed, 1 2 O.R. wounded.	JP

J.A. Garnett Lieut Col
1/4th Bn Suffolk Regt.

Army Form C. 2118.

WAR DIARY
or
INTELLIGENCE SUMMARY.   4th SUFFOLK REGT

(Erase heading not required.)

Instructions regarding War Diaries and Intelligence Summaries are contained in F.S. Regs., Part II. and the Staff Manual respectively. Title pages will be prepared in manuscript.

Place	Date	Hour	Summary of Events and Information	Remarks and references to Appendices
RONGY	Nov 6th		Work as usual. District shelled at intervals both by day & night. Casualties 2 O.R. wounded. Capt A.R. GEYER. R.A.M.C. was attached to the battalion for duty.	IP
RONGY	Nov 7th		Work continued. The late Capt J. GASTON M.C. R.A.M.C. was buried with military honours in the churchyard at RUMEGIES. During the day the district was heavily shelled & general.	IP
RONGY	Nov 8th		Enemy withdrew on Divisional front. All Coy at work on tidying canal. "D" Coy moved into billets at RONGY on completion of days work. Weather very wet.	It
RONGY	Nov 9th		Battalion less "B" Coy moved to billets in ROSULT. "B" Coy moved to BLÉHARIES. Coys worked at tidying & repair of roads.	IP

Lt Colonel
H/Bn Suffolk Regt

WAR DIARY
or
INTELLIGENCE SUMMARY.   4TH SUFFOLK REGT
(Erase heading not required.)

Army Form C. 2118.

Place	Date	Hour	Summary of Events and Information	Remarks and references to Appendices
ROUEX	Nov 10th		Left ROUEX at 9.45 A.M. & marched to WIERS. On completion of work all Coy billeted there. Town en fête on account of the evacuation of the enemy & prospect of armistice.	T.R.
WIERS	Nov 11th		Left WIERS at 9.20 A.M. & marched to BASECLES arriving 12 noon. A + B Coy joined H.Qu. there on completion of work. D Coy working forward billeted in BELOEIL. At 11 A.M. Germany having agreed to accept the conditions for an Armistice as laid down by the Allies & hostilities ceased at that hour.	T.R.
BASECLES	Nov 12th		"D" Coy continued work at BELOEIL. Remainder rested	T.R.
BASECLES	Nov 13th		"A" Coy worked on road to LA BOITERIE, "B" Coy on railway line at BASECLES, "D" Coy on bridge over canal W of BELOEIL.	T.R.
BASECLES	Nov 14th		Marched to billets at ECACHERIES starting at 11 A.M. & arriving 1.10 P.M. Here we were joined by "D" Coy. Suffolk Regt. 1st Lieut B. WEBB awarded the Military Cross.	T.R.

For O. in Command 4th Coy
4/Bn Suffolk Regt

Army Form C. 2118.

WAR DIARY
or
INTELLIGENCE SUMMARY.
(Erase heading not required.)

Instructions regarding War Diaries and Intelligence Summaries are contained in F. S. Regs., Part II. and the Staff Manual respectively. Title pages will be prepared in manuscript.

Place	Date	Hour	Summary of Events and Information	Remarks and references to Appendices
ECACHERIES	Nov 15th		Coy attached to Field Coy R.E. & worked on road craters & bridge.	T.F.
ECACHERIES	Nov 16th		Work continued in conjunction with R.E.	T.F.
ECACHERIES	Nov 17th		H.Q & "B" Coy Church parade at 11:30 A.M. Remainder at work on roads & bridge.	T.F.
ECACHERIES	Nov 18th		Work continued. Lieut. F.H. WOODCOCK rejoined for duty.	T.F.
ECACHERIES	Nov 19th		"A" Coy worked in conjunction with R.E. "B" Coy training in morning. Football in afternoon. Class for elementary instruction in reading, writing & arithmetic commenced.	T.F.
ECACHERIES	Nov 20th		Coy Parade for 2 hours in morning. Elementary class continued & a short-hand class formed. Football in afternoon.	T.F.

Lieut Col
4th Bn Suffolk Regt

Army Form C. 2118.

WAR DIARY
or
INTELLIGENCE SUMMARY. 4TH SUFFOLK REGT
(Erase heading not required.)

Instructions regarding War Diaries and Intelligence Summaries are contained in F. S. Regs., Part II. and the Staff Manual respectively. Title pages will be prepared in manuscript.

Place	Date	Hour	Summary of Events and Information	Remarks and references to Appendices
ECACHERIES	Nov 21st		Coy training in morning. Football in afternoon. Educational classes continued.	T.P.
ECACHERIES	Nov 22nd		Coy training & Battalion parade in morning. Football in afternoon. Lecture on INDIA by C.O. in evening.	T.P.
ECACHERIES	Nov 23rd		Coy training & Battalion parade in morning. Football in afternoon.	T.P.
ECACHERIES	Nov 24th		Church parade 10.A.M	T.P.
ECACHERIES	Nov 25th		Coy training in morning. Football & cross-country running in afternoon. Educational classes continued.	T.P.

In command Lieut Col
4th Suffolk Regt

Army Form C. 2118.

WAR DIARY
or
INTELLIGENCE SUMMARY.
(Erase heading not required.)

4TH SUFFOLK REGT

Instructions regarding War Diaries and Intelligence Summaries are contained in F.S. Regs., Part II. and the Staff Manual respectively. Title pages will be prepared in manuscript.

Place	Date	Hour	Summary of Events and Information	Remarks and references to Appendices
ECACHERIES	Nov 26TH		Battalion drill in morning. Football in afternoon. Educational classes continued	TR
ECACHERIES	Nov 27TH		Coy training in morning. Games in afternoon. Educational classes in progress in the following subjects:- Elementary Class, Bookkeeping, English, French, Shorthand. Lieut C.H. HUME found for duty	TR
ECACHERIES	Nov 28TH		Coy training followed by battalion drill in morning. Football etc in afternoon	TR
ECACHERIES	Nov 29TH		Battalion route march in morning. Football matches & educational classes proceeded with. Capt H.C. HENLEY joined for duty	TR

1/2 Commanding Regt Col
4/5 Br Suffolk Regt

Army Form C. 2118.

WAR DIARY
or
INTELLIGENCE SUMMARY.   4ᵀᴴ SUFFOLK Rᴱᴳᵀ

(Erase heading not required.)

Instructions regarding War Diaries and Intelligence Summaries are contained in F. S. Regs., Part II, and the Staff Manual respectively. Title pages will be prepared in manuscript.

Place	Date	Hour	Summary of Events and Information	Remarks and references to Appendices
ECACHERIES	Nov 30ᵗʰ		Battalion ceremonial drill in morning. Football matches in afternoon. Educational classes continued	7B

Lt Gammon
Lieut Col
4th Bn Suffolk Regt

Headquarters,
    58th Division.

       Herewith War Diary of this Battalion for December, 1918.

       Will you please acknowledge receipt.

                                                   Lieut. Col.,
                          Commdg. 4th Bn Suffolk Regiment.

4TH BATTALION,
SUFFOLK
REGIMENT.
No. K.A.426.
Date 6/1/19.

A.G's BRANCH
G.H.Q. 3rd ECHELON
RECEIVED.

CAPTAIN,
for D.A.G.

DATE

Army Form C. 2118.

WAR DIARY
or
INTELLIGENCE SUMMARY.
(Erase heading not required.)

4TH SUFFOLK REGT

Vol 40

Place	Date	Hour	Summary of Events and Information	Remarks and references to Appendices
ETACHERIES	Dec 1st		The battalion marched to STABRUGES & attended divine service in the Cinema Hall	7.P.
ETACHERIES	Dec 2nd		Left huts at 8.50 hrs & marched to the aviation ground at GRANDGLISE where General Sir H. S. HORNE. K.C.B. K.C.M.G Commanding the first Army inspected the 58th Division at 11.00 hrs. The inspection concluded with a march past & the G. O. C. Army expressed his satisfaction at the steadiness, turn out of men troops. Football in the afternoon.	7.P.
ETACHERIES	Dec 3rd		Parade under Company commander in morning. Football in afternoon. Educational training continued	7.P
ETACHERIES	Dec 4th		Battalion route march in morning. Football in afternoon. Educational training as usual.	7.P

F. A. Groom
Comdg 4th Suffolk Regt
Lieut Col

Army Form C. 2118.

WAR DIARY
of
INTELLIGENCE SUMMARY.   4TH SUFFOLK REGT

(Erase heading not required.)

Instructions regarding War Diaries and Intelligence Summaries are contained in F.S. Regs., Part II. and the Staff Manual respectively. Title pages will be prepared in manuscript.

Place	Date	Hour	Summary of Events and Information	Remarks and references to Appendices
ECACHERIES	Dec 5th		H.M. THE KING drove through the area occupied by the 58th Division. The battalion assembled at a point EAST of STAMBRUGES to watch him go by + the Troops were enthusiastically cheered by all as he passed by.	7P
ECACHERIES	Dec 6th		Coy training in morning. Football & inter-coy. country run in afternoon. Educational classes continued.	7P
ECACHERIES	Dec 7th		Short route march in morning. Football in afternoon.	7P
ECACHERIES	Dec 8th		Battalion marched to BELŒIL in morning, & attended divine service in the Cinema Hall. Lieut G.B. BANNERMAN rejoined the battalion	7P
ECACHERIES	Dec 9th		Coy parades in morning. Football in afternoon. Educational classes continued.	7P

In absence of Field Ont
Comdy 4/Bn Suffolk Regt

Army Form C. 2118.

WAR DIARY
or
INTELLIGENCE SUMMARY. 4TH SUFFOLK REGT

(Erase heading not required.)

Instructions regarding War Diaries and Intelligence
Summaries are contained in F. S. Regs., Part II.
and the Staff Manual respectively. Title pages
will be prepared in manuscript.

Place	Date	Hour	Summary of Events and Information	Remarks and references to Appendices
ECACHERIES	Dec 10th/18		Coy parade in morning. Football in afternoon. Educational classes continued	A.P.
ECACHERIES	Dec 11th/18		Rain interfered with out-door work. Educational classes continued	A.P.
ECACHERIES	Dec 12th/18		"A" Coy moved to MAULDE for work under C.R.E. Weather very wet. Armourer Sergt inspected rifles. Educational classes as usual.	A.P.
ECACHERIES	Dec 13th/18		Parades under Coy arrangements. Educational classes as usual	A.P.
ECACHERIES	Dec 14th/18		Coy parades & baths. Educational classes as usual	A.P.

In Command 4th Suffolk Regt
Comdg 4th Bn Suffolk Regt

Army Form C. 2118.

WAR DIARY
or
INTELLIGENCE SUMMARY.   4TH SUFFOLK REGT

(Erase heading not required.)

Instructions regarding War Diaries and Intelligence Summaries are contained in F.S. Regs., Part II. and the Staff Manual respectively. Title pages will be prepared in manuscript.

Place	Date	Hour	Summary of Events and Information	Remarks and references to Appendices
ECACHERIES	Dec 15th		Battalion marched to BELLOIL & attended divine service in the cinema Hall	F.P.
ECACHERIES	Dec 16th		Played 2/12th London Regt at football in afternoon, result 4-0 in our favour.	P.S.P.
			Coy Parades. Educational Classes as usual. Football in the afternoon.	P.S.P.
ECACHERIES	Dec 17		Short route march in the morning. Football in the afternoon. Lecture by the C.O. on "India" in the evening	P.S.P.
ECACHERIES	Dec 18		Coy Parades. Educational Classes continued. Football match revs 1st 2nd Battalion Regt. cancelled owing to Bad weather.	P.S.P.
ECACHERIES	Dec 19		Coy Parades as usual. Lecture by M.G. in the evening	P.S.P.
Dec 20			Bn. moved to STAMBRUGES. Spent the day in cleaning billets	P.S.P.
STAMBRUGES	Dec 21		Coy Parades. Bn went to WATER at BELLOIL. Educational Classes resumed.	P.S.P.
STAMBRUGES	Dec. 22		Coy Parades. Bn rejoined the Bath from MAULDE.	P.S.P.
STAMBRUGES	Dec 23		Coy Parades as usual. Educational Classes discontinued until after Xmas	P.S.P.
STAMBRUGES	Dec 24		No Parades. Bn Concert Party gave an entertainment in the evening	P.S.P.
STAMBRUGES	Dec 25		Bn Church Parade in the morning. Cinema in Queen's Cinema in afternoon	P.S.P.
STAMBRUGES	Dec 26		Bn Football match vs 7th D.A. Column result; draw 2 goals each.	P.S.P.

J.A. Greene Lt Col
Comdg 4th Bn Suffolk Regt

WAR DIARY
INTELLIGENCE SUMMARY
(Erase heading not required.)

Army Form C. 2118.

4th Bn Suffolk Regt

Place	Date	Hour	Summary of Events and Information	Remarks and references to Appendices
STAMBRUGES	24/h Dec		Coy Parades. Running all day. Educational Classes resumed	equa.
"	28th "		Coy Parades. Running. Educational Classes.	equa.
"	29th "		Coy Parades. Running.	equa.
"	30th "		Coy Parades. Football in the afternoon. Educational Classes as usual.	equa.
"	31st "		Working party of 1 Officer and 25 men proceeded to QUEVAUCAMPS and another party of 3 Officers and 56 Other Ranks left for MAUBE under command of Capt. HENLEY.	equa.

J.R. Cooper
Lieut Col.
Comdg 4th Bn Suffolk Regt.

SECRET

Headquarters 14
58th Division

Akrewich War Diary
of the Battalion for
January 1919.

P G Parr
Capt & Adjt
for Lieut Col
Comdg Suffolk Regt

4TH BATTALION.
SUFFOLK
REGIMENT.
No. KA491
Date 12.2.19

Army Form C. 2118.

WAR DIARY
or
INTELLIGENCE SUMMARY.
(Erase heading not required.)

4th BN SUFFOLK REGT. (T.F.)

Place	Date	Hour	Summary of Events and Information	Remarks and references to Appendices
STAMBRUGES	1919 Jan	1	Parades under Coy arrangements. Educational classes as usual. Route march in morning	Appx A
"	"	2	"	Appx A
"	"	3	Football at Beloeil. Won	Appx A
"	"	4	Coy Parades	Appx A
"	"	5		Appx A
"	"	6	The Bn marches to QUEVAUCAMPS to attend Divine Service. Parades under Coy arrangements. Educational classes continue. Lecture in the evening	Appx A
"	"	7	Parades under Coy arrangements. Educational classes as usual. Cinema show under Regimental arrangements in the evening	Appx A
"	"	8	Bn route march in morning. Educational classes continue	Appx A
"	"	9	Parades under Coy arrangements. Educational classes continue. Lecture in evening on Agriculture by Capt Taylor	Appx A
"	"	10	Parades under Coy arrangements. Educational classes continued in the evening	Appx A
"	"	11	Parades under Coy arrangements. Exercise classes continue. On Range the 12th London Regt at Grenier Bois but turnout was by 1 pm as at Tank Bridge to an O.R.S. demobiliza	Appx A

J. R. Greenwood Lieut Col
O/mdg 4th Bn Suffolk Regt.

Army Form C. 2118.

WAR DIARY
INTELLIGENCE SUMMARY.
(Erase heading not required.)

4 T. Bn Suffolk Regt (TF)

Place	Date	Hour	Summary of Events and Information	Remarks and references to Appendices
STAMBRUGES	1919 Jan 12		Bn assembled for Divine Service in Cinema Hall. The Bn 2nd XI played the 310 Coy R.A.S.C. at football at QUEVAUCAMPS result the home team won by 3 goals to nil. 2 O.R's demobilised.	E.W.S.A.
"	13		The Bn attended the Baths at BELOEIL. Educational classes continue. A football match with the 310 Coy R.A.S.C. resulted in a win for the R.A.S.C. by 4 goals to nil.	E.W.S.A.
"	14		Parade under Coy arrangements. Educational classes as usual. Cinema show in the evening.	E.W.S.A.
"	15		Companies carried out the usual company training. Educational classes as usual. Twenty eight O.R's join the Bn as reinforcements. Sgt. Smith and Lance/Cpl. Head awarded Belgian Decorations. The 9/Cd Z concert party gave a performance in the evening.	E.W.S.A.
"	16		Parades under Company arrangements. Educational classes continue.	E.W.S.A.
"	17		Battalion route march in morning also Battalion classes. The Battalion Jnr. H.Wt. War team won the contest with the R.A.S.C. at LEUZE	E.W.S.A.
"	18		Company Parades and Education classes in morning. The team played the 58th D.A.C. at STAMBRUGES in the afternoon losing by 4 goals to 2. 2 O.R's demobilised.	E.W.S.A.

John Officer Capt & am. Lieut. Colonel
Comdg 4 Bn Suffolk Regt

Army Form C. 2118.

WAR DIARY
INTELLIGENCE SUMMARY

(Erase heading not required.)

4TH BN SUFFOLK REGT (T.F.)

Instructions regarding War Diaries and Intelligence Summaries are contained in F. S. Regs., Part II. and the Staff Manual respectively. Title pages will be prepared in manuscript.

Place	Date	Hour	Summary of Events and Information	Remarks and references to Appendices
STAMBRUGES	1919 Jan. 19		Bn assembled for Divine Service in Cinema Hall. 2 O.R's Demobilised.	Appx. A.
"	" 20		On attached the Bn at BELOEIL. Educational classes continued. In Bn 2nd Lt. Pemper the 51st. By R.A.S.C., 2nd Lt. STANBRIDGES going by 19th Bn. 2nd Lt. Themas to 133rd Siege Battery.	Appx. A.
"	" 21		Parades under Company arrangements and Educational classes continued.	Appx. A.
"	" 22		Parades under Company arrangements and 4 O.R's to Sept. C.R.E. Temp W.F. Delay and Sergt. Fife. Machine Gun. School turned to Cinema film in the evening	
"	" 23		Coy. English. Regular program of Cinema films in the evening. Parade under Company arrangements and Educational classes continued. The 291 Bdgs R.F.A. Troups "Trumps" gave a Performance in the evening	G. A.W.A.
"	" 24		The usual Company Parades and Educational classes the Pon Sug. of war team won the Divisional tournament.	Appx. A.
"	" 25		The usual Company Parades and Educational classes. Special Orders by the C.O. "A Farewell". 13 O.R's Demobilised also 2nd Lt. I.H. Cooper.	Appx. A.
"	" 26		On assembled for Divine Service in Cinema Hall. Snowing all day. 25 O.R's Demobilised, 4 H.L. D.R's. Delay	Appx. A.
"	" 27		No Parades, but the usual Educational classes. 13 O.R's Demobilised.	Appx. A.
"	" 28		The Other Ranks not Church engaged Parades to Church and March. 13 O.R's Demobilised. Peace of Gen. Monday. Captain and M.C.S. of M.G.C. Bond Supply 82	Appx. A.
"	" 29			Appx. A.
"	" 30		First took march and Educational classes 10 O.R's Demobilised.	Appx. A.
"	" 31		Bn Ran for the Rice children Xmas Funds. Bn arrived march to GRANDGLISE. Educational classes.	Appx. A.

D. D. & L., London, B.C. (A8001) Wt. W1771/M2031 750,000 5/17 Sch. 82 Forms/C2118/14

WAR DIARY or INTELLIGENCE SUMMARY

Army Form C. 2118.

1/3 4 Suffolk Rgt
Vol 4 L2

Place	Date	Hour	Summary of Events and Information	Remarks and references to Appendices
STANBRIDGES	1st Feb.		Bn Baths at GRANDGLISE. Lecture by the C.O. "Navigation". 10 O.R's Demobilized. Educational classes continued	P.J.P.
"	2nd Feb.		Bn at the Cinema in Jemma Hall at 11.30 hours.	P.J.P.
"	3rd Feb.		21 O.R's Demobilized. Coy Parades for Physical Drill & Short Route March	P.J.P.
"	4th Feb.		10 O.R's Demobilized. Coy parades as usual. Educational classes continued	P.J.P.
"	5th Feb.		Coy parades as usual	P.J.P.
"	6th Feb.		Coy parades for drill etc. 2/Lt Hargreaves D 15 O.R's Demobilized.	P.J.P.
"	7th Feb.		Bn Dcy & Bn H.Q. Staff at GRANDGLISE. Remainder of Bn cleaning up village. 10 O.R's Demobilized.	P.J.P.
"	8th Feb.		Bn Dcy & McDeroch & 10 O.R's. A & D Coy. Remainder of Bn employed in cleaning up village. Lecture "Geography" by the C.O. at 11.00 hours.	P.J.P.
"	9th Feb.		Bn attended Divine Service in the Cinema at 11.00 hours.	P.J.P.
"	10th Feb.		Coy parades as usual under Coy arrangements.	P.J.P.
"	11th Feb.		14 O.R's Demobilized. Coy parades under Coy arrangements. Educational classes continued	P.J.P.
"	12th Feb.		Coy parades as usual. D Coy moved to their billets in same village to be vacated by them.	P.J.P.
"	13th Feb.		Coy parade. Spent morning cleaning billets. C.O.'s Lecture on the "Mining of Australia". 16 O.R's Demobilized. Sir Cunninghame	P.J.P.

Army Form C. 2118.

WAR DIARY
INTELLIGENCE SUMMARY.
(Erase heading not required.)

Instructions regarding War Diaries and Intelligence Summaries are contained in F. S. Regs., Part II. and the Staff Manual respectively. Title pages will be prepared in manuscript.

Place	Date	Hour	Summary of Events and Information	Remarks and references to Appendices
STAMBRUGES	14	Feb.	Coy parades as usual, under Coy arrangements. Educational classes	P.g.P.
"	15	Feb.	as usual. 2 Coy's demobilized.	P.g.P.
"	15	Feb.	Bn. bathed at GRANDGLISE. 16 O.R's demobilized.	P.g.P.
"	16	Feb.	Bn. Church Parade in the morning. 16 O.R's demobilized.	P.g.P.
"	17	Feb.	Sig. Hundecourt P. awarded M.M.	
"	17	Feb.	Bn. Route March in the morning. Educational Classes continued.	P.g.P.
"	18	Feb.	14 O.R. demobilized. Coy arrangements. Educational classes.	
"	19	Feb.	Parades for Physical Training, arms drill	
"	20	Feb.	Coy Parades. 15 O.R's demobilized & Educational classes.	
"	21	Feb.	Bn. bathed at GRANDGLISE. 44 O.R's demobilized	
"	22	Feb.	Coy parades under Coy arrangts. 15 O.R's demobilized.	
"	23	Feb.	Voluntary Church Service. 49 O.R's demobilized.	
"	24	Feb.	Coy Parades under Coy Arrangements	
"	25	Feb.	Above. Parades for Instruction by Company Officer.	
"	26	Feb.	Do.	
"	27		Do.	
"	28		Coy Garrison under Coy Arrangements. 22 L.H. Herme & 20 O.R's demobilized	

J. Gilman
Lieut. Col.
Commdg 4th Bn. Inf.R.R Regt.

ATTACHED

RHINE ARMY
EASTERN DIVISION
(LATE 34TH DIVISION)

4TH BN SUFFOLK REGIMENT
MAR - JLY 1919

2866

Army Form C. 2118.

1/4th Bn Suffolk Regt. (T.F.)

WAR DIARY
INTELLIGENCE SUMMARY
(Erase heading not required.)

Instructions regarding War Diaries and Intelligence Summaries are contained in F.S. Regs., Part II. and the Staff Manual respectively. Title pages will be prepared in manuscript.

Place	Date	Hour	Summary of Events and Information	Remarks and references to Appendices
STAMBRUGES	1st March		Company Parades as usual under Coy arrangements. 40 O.R's 58% Durham Interned appointed Bn.	R.J.P
"	2nd "		Battalion proceeded to LEUZE at 10.00 hrs. arriving at 1.15 hrs. Bn. placed in billets for night prior to entraining for Army of Occupation.	R.J.P
LEUZE	3rd "		Battalion entrained for TROISDORF GERMANY.	R.J.P
"	4th "		Train stopped at VERVIERS where tea was served to all ranks. Arrived at TROISDORF 16.45 hrs.	R.J.P
TROISDORF	5th		Working Party of 10 O.R's reported to Corps R.E. DUMP. 2/Lieut Z.R. Abbott struck off Strength on being evacuated to England 4/3/19.	R.J.P
"	6th "		Working Party of 1 Officer + 50 O.R's reported to R.E. DUMP. The G.O.C. 34th Division addressed all Officers of Battalion.	R.J.P
"	7th "			R.J.P
"	8th "		Working Party of 1 Officer + 25 O.R's reported to R.E. DUMP.	R.J.P
"	9th "		R.E. Dump P: 6 B.Rect 1/1st Hertford Regt attached 16 Bn. Voluntary Church Service Lt. G.G. Bowerman struck off strength on proceeding to England. 16 Officers + 176 O.R's of 2/8th Bn. Suffolk Regt. joined this Bn. as reinforcements and were taken on Strength with effect as from 9/3/19.	R.J.P
"	10th		Working Parties as for previous days. Lieut T.H. Blomfield struck off Strength on proceeding to England. Must effect as from 19/3/19.	R.J.P
"	11th		Working Parties as per previous days.	R.J.P
"	12th		Major T. Servington appointed 2nd in Command of the Batt. as from 12.3.19. Capt Sergeant assumed temporary Command of "B" Coy. Vice Major T. Servington. Working Parties as per previous days. 16 O.R's returned the Batta. as reinforcements as from the 12th.	R.J.P

Army Form C. 2118.

WAR DIARY
or
INTELLIGENCE SUMMARY.
(Erase heading not required.)

1st Bn Suffolk Regt. (T)

Place	Date	Hour	Summary of Events and Information	Remarks and references to Appendices
TROISDORF	13th March		Major S. Pennington M.C. assumed command of the Battalion as from 14.3.19.	
	14th		7 Officers & joined the Batt: as reinforcements 2nd Lieut to be by-walking offer. 1 Officer 50 OR's Infantry R.E. Dumps. D. Coy began nts fillers in S. wing of Artillery R.S.B. 2 ORs joined the Battalion for duty and posted to B Coy.	
	15th		C.O.'s inspection of all reinforcements from the 1st Suffolk Regiment at 11.00hrs. 10 Off 50 ORs working party report to R.E. Dumps. Capt L. Knight M.C. assumed command of "D" Coy vice Lieut Atkinson? Major Ashton M.C.C.M. to be Asst./Adjt./ as from the 16th.	P.S.P.
	16th		Batt attended Divine Service in the M.E.C. Cinema at 11.00hrs. From today the 34th Divn is re-named EASTERN DIVISION. 5 Off 150 ORs of the 7th Bn Northants joined this Battn as reinforcements and are taken on the strength with effect as from the 16th/3/1919.	P.S.P.
	17th		G.O.C. EASTERN Divn inspected the Battn at 12.30 hrs:	
	18th		C.O. inspected draft of 150 ORs (7th Northants) at 11.00am. Working party of 2 Off 100 ORants reported to R.E. Dumps. Tournant	P.S.P.
	19th		Usual working party 2 Off 100 ORs supplied. C.G. present under Coy arrangements.	P.S.P.
	20th		Usual working parties supplied 50 ORants under w/R.E. Dumps P.S.P. Company Parades under Coy arrangements	P.S.P.

Army Form C. 2118.

WAR DIARY
or
INTELLIGENCE SUMMARY.
(Erase heading not required.)

H Bn Suffolk Regt (T.)

Place	Date	Hour	Summary of Events and Information	Remarks and references to Appendices
Troisdorf	21.3.19		Working parties of 1 officer 30 O.Rs outpost for works at R.E. Dump. Coys paraded Platoon drill & arrangements	P.Q.P.
"	22.3.19		Working party 20/s 30 ORs for work at R.E. Dump. "B" Coy 1 plat of "A" Coy at 10-30 hrs. Left JDA hut. MEA train Rn R.to parade rpt H.Q. 3 offrs. Strength of the Battn on Parade 21/3/19	P.Q.P.
"	23.3.19		Battn paraded for Church service. The MGC (Yeoca) accompanied at 10.30 hrs	P.Q.P.
"	24.3.19		Company parades usual arrangements	P.Q.P.
"	25.3.19		Working parties of 3 officers 60 ORs for work on R.E. Dumps	P.Q.P.
"	26.3.19		Coys parades usual L.G. Corp 2 offrs 162 ORs joined the Battn as 40th reinforcement from the 15th Suffolk Regt	P.Q.P. 40 B.
"	27.3.19		C.O. inspected draft from the 15th Suffolk Regt. Working parties of 2 officers 50 ORs reported for 2 Dumps for work. Coys parades usual arrangements	P.Q.P.
"	28.3.19		Coys paraded as usual. 1 Sunne of "A" Coy for instructions 2.30 2 Offrs 50 ORs Coys working parties for work at R.E. Dumps. Capt H. Scott Walker MC Cozens command of "A" Coy vice A/Major CP Perry Croker returned to England for demobilization.	P.Q.P.

S. Perry
Comdg H Suffolk Regt.

WAR DIARY
or
INTELLIGENCE SUMMARY.

Army Form C. 2118.

4th Bn Suffolk Regt (T.F.)

Place	Date	Hour	Summary of Events and Information	Remarks and references to Appendices
TROISDORF	29 March 1919		Inter Coy football (Knock-out) competition. 50 ORs for work as at R.E. Dump TROISDORF. C.O. inspected Church of "D" Coy in the morning. At Divine Service attended letter of T.O. was distributed to U.K. for demob. "A" Coy party under 2/Lt L.G. WEBB were detailed in assistance with the afternoon duty. To organise stage fixtures for theatrical affairs for coming evening.	P.3. P
"	30/3/19		Bath attended Divine Service at 10:30hr at the H.Q.S. Cinema. Trooping 100 O.Rs left the Battn for movements to Depôt Coys R.E.	P.3.
"	31/3/19		Coys paraded under own arrangements. 1 gunner of "B" Coy under L/S Gpcw working party of 2 officers and 50 orders reported for work at R.E. Dumps, TROISDORF.	P.3.

S. [signature]
Major.
Commdg 4th Bn Suffolk Regt.

D. A. G.
G. H. Q.
  3rd Echelon.

April 1919.

Herewith War Diary of this Battalion for

[Stamp: BATTALION SUFFOLK REGIMENT. No. B.S. 14. 7/5/19.]

S.E. Knapp Lt & A/Adjt

Lieut. Col...
Commanding 4th Bn. The Suffolk Regiment.

WAR DIARY
or
INTELLIGENCE SUMMARY.
(Erase heading not required.)

Army Form C. 2118.

Place	Date	Hour	Summary of Events and Information	Remarks and references to Appendices
TROISDORF (Cologne)	1st April 1919		Training under Company Commrs. - The following Officers joined the Battn. from 11th Suffolks Capt. H.A. REDDING, M.C., Capt. F. ADAMS, Lieut. T.E. GOOCH, 2/Lieut. E. MARSH, W.J. HUNT, G.K. SILLS.	
	2nd		" Colby H.C. HENLEY and 2/Lt. J.H. WAKELEY. Who embd. for home. Lecture by Capt. E.G. ADAMS Canada. Her Trade & Resources	
	3rd		Inter Platoon Football Competition. Lieut. W.H.F. BRIERLEY joined Bn.	
	4 II		Company Training.	
	5		"	
	6th		" Capt. H.A. REDDING & 9 ORs assumed command of G.B. Coy vice Lt.A/Capt. HOWDEN 2/Lt. H.W. HUNT joined Battalion.	
			Bn. Major (T. LATHAM of C. STUBBS DSO) assumed command of Batt. vice Lt Col. A.C. LOGMAN CMG DSO	
	6th		Church Parade. One Battn Officers Mess formed for whole Battn.	
	7		Company Training - Inspection of Transport by Col. FALLMAN. Officers Joined Battn - Capt. E.V. MULLIS, 2/Lieut G.F.L. PELHAM, Lieut S.E. KNAPP.	
			Lt. DAVIDSON appointed Battn Educn. Officer with 3 Officer Asst Instructs & 8 NCOs	
			Asst Instrs - 1 Officer & 1 NCO to supervise each Coy. All coys to do 1 hr Education a day - Special combined class formed Std I scale thin	
			attend 2 1/2 hrs running per day - Platoon Cmdrs to be responsible for the	
	8th		Instruction of their Platoons in General Subjects have assisted by Education Officer & staff.	
			Battn Football - lecture by Capt. WEATHERHEAD in Temperance	
	9		by Trim Maj. Lt. T.R.K. GINGER, MC joined Battn.	

WAR DIARY
or
INTELLIGENCE SUMMARY

Army Form C. 2118.

Place	Date	Hour	Summary of Events and Information	Remarks and references to Appendices
TROISDORF	April 10		Company Training. Lect f/b STANFORD 2nd i/c & O.C.F. PELHAM BURN killed – C.O. Inspected Batt?	S.D.F.
	11		Company Training – lecture by C.O. "Attacking" – to Officers & NCOs – Officers v Sergts Assoc Football – (3-3)	S.D.F.
	12		at Assoc Football – (3-3)	S.D.F.
	13		Church Parade –	S.D.F.
	14		Company Training –	S.D.F.
	15		Inspection of A Coy in Marching order. Sent find of telephones For Coms Bonat. Requires repairs to deal in Battalions Equipments.	S.D.F.
	16		Inspection of B Coy by C.O. in Marching order. 2/Lieut T. BOURNE joins Batt? Batt? play C? at Field Met at Soccer.	S.D.F.
	17		Inspection of D Coy by C.O. in Marching order – "B" Coy beat by Sports	S.D.F.
	18		Church parade – Batt? play H.Q. Coy Easter Div. R.A.S.C. Lieut N.A. Ellson rejoins Batt?	S.D.F.
	19		Batt? Ceremonial parade.	S.D.F.
	20		Church Parade – 2/Lieut (T/Capt) W.G. Bates D.S.O. & C. joined from 2nd Batt?	S.D.F.
	21		Easter Monday observed as a Holiday – Lt Col (A/B?n) F.S. Gabot R.E. Sutherland	S.D.F.
	22		rejoined on completion of course at S.O.S. Aldershot & assumed duty as 2nd i/c Company Training –	S.D.F.

D.D. & I, London, E.C.
(A8001) Wt. W17711/M2031 750,000 5/17 Sch. 52 Forms/C2-2118/14

WAR DIARY or INTELLIGENCE SUMMARY

Army Form C. 2118.

Place	Date	Hour	Summary of Events and Information	Remarks and references to Appendices
TROISDORF	1919 April 23rd		St George's Day. All ranks wore Roses or flags on tunics. Officers Bats- Lt Col Nicholson Commanding. Easter D.V. inspected & his billets in the Potteries.	SS/1
	24		Factory training was carried on as usual. All officers ordered to carry revolvers at all times owing to rumoured Bolshevist plot— Training as usual— Battn Baths	SS/2
	25		Training interrupted by rain— HQ held sports after noon.	SS/1
	26		Battn drill under Bn. Lieut.— The following Officers were posted to 11th Suffolks. Capt K. Scott-Walker, M.C., Lieuts H. Williamson, W.G. Gentle, M.C., H.A. Edwards, W.F. Brierley, R.E. Gooch, H., R. Horth, E.C. Mogridge, 2/Lieuts H.G.H. Perks, E.L. Broadbridge, H.W. Hunt, W.H.A. Stenning, R.O.S. Kettle, H.J. Avery, J. Bourne, H.C. Manly.	SS/1
	27		Church parade.	
	28		Training as usual— 'A' Coy held Sports afternoon— 2/Lieut J.R. Cutley joined Battn from 11th Suffolk.	SS/1
	29		General Sir W. Robertson C-in-C. of British Army of Rhine inspected Battn at S. Egburg— Dress marching order— Leave allotment increased to 14 O.R per day—	SS/1
	30		Company Training & Battn Baths—	SS/1

6.5.19

G.C. Stubbs Lt Col
Comdg 4th Suffolk Regt

Army Form C. 2118.

4TH BATTALION
SUFFOLK
REGIMENT.

WAR DIARY
or
INTELLIGENCE SUMMARY.
(Erase heading not required.)

4th Bn Suffolk Regt (T.F.)

Place	Date	Hour	Summary of Events and Information	Remarks and references to Appendices
TROISDORF	1st May 1919		AT.B Coys were detailed in special garrison duty in case of any German Palms trouble. Packing & Kit Stores at the Monastery. B Coy were all housing in reserve for day.	
	2 " "		ATB Coys returned for Serg. burg at 10.00hrs. Football match at 14.30 hrs Batt v M.G.C. Result Batt o M.G.C. 1. Showery.	
	3 " "		Head working party. Coys under Company Commands in training. Fine & warm.	
	4 " "		Church Parade at the Cinema. Football match at 14.30 hrs Batt v M.G.C. Result Batt o M.G.C. 1. Very warm.	
	5 " "		Head working party. Coys under Coy arrangements. A/Lt went on leave. Cricket match officers v NCO's. Result 132 for 6 wkts NCO's 52. Lecture by Canon Maynock (subject "Life.") Announcement of A Armour. Coys under Coy arrangements. F Coy sports 14 hrs. Batt hockey match v R.W. Kent. Result Batt 4. R.W.K. 1. Fine.	
	6 " "		Battle for the Batt.	
	7 " "		Coys under Coy arrangements. Hockey match. Batt v Brown. Result Batt's 2nd 4.	
	8 " "		Coys under Coy arrangements. Batt Football match 14.30 hrs v the 7.A.	
	9 " "		Result Batt ? F.A.1. Lecture by ?	
	10 " "		Coys under Coy arrangements. 7 Batt Hockey match v M.G.C. Result Batt 4. M.G.C. 1.	
	11 " "		Church Parade at the Cinema.	
	12 " "		Head working party. Coys under their own arrangements.	

E.W.Foss
Lt. Colonel,
Commanding 4th Bn. Suffolk Regt.

Army Form C. 2118

WAR DIARY or INTELLIGENCE SUMMARY
(Erase heading not required.)

4TH BATTALION. SUFFOLK REGIMENT.

H.Q. 4th Bn Suffolk Regt (T.F.)

Place	Date	Hour	Summary of Events and Information	Remarks and references to Appendices
TROISDORF	13.5.19		Company training. Manual working party to R.E.s. Lecture by Rev. Colwyn. F.S. Dupen. Bicey. Subject:- "Some Problems of Democracy." Cricket Match at 14.30 hrs. H.Q.B. Coys V D Coy H.Q.	
	14.5.19		Parade – Ceremonial. Commanding Officers Parade as strong as possible. The Colours which have arrived from England were inspected on parade. Company training. Working party to R.E.s. Advance party of D Coy moved to HERKENRATH.	
	15.5.19		Company training. Working party to R.E.s.	
	16.5.19		D. Coy moved at 0630 hrs to HERKENRATH to concentrate. A & B. Company training. Working party to R.E.s. Lecture by Rev J. R. Bate. Subject:- "Beautiful Scenery of the Rhine area."	
	17.5.19		Company training. Working party to R.E.s. Lecture by Rev J. R. Bate. Subject:- "Beautiful Scenery of the Rhine area."	
	18.5.19		Church Service at 11.30 hrs in Herenrath Room. Powder Factory	
	19.5.19		Company training. Working party to R.E.s.	
	20.5.19		Company training. Working party to R.E.s.	
	21.5.19		Battn. lecture at 13.30 M.E.C. on "Bolshevism" by Capt Lydon. Drawn up apart for the Cadre of 2nd Bn. Suffolk Regiment from OPPES Station en route for ALVERINGT.	
	22.5.19		Company training. Working party to R.E.s. 21 Oman + 32 OR. I Coy proceeded to WAHN for work on the Artillery Ranges.	

R.C.S.(illegible)
Lt. Colonel,
Commanding 4th Bn. Suffolk Regt.

Army Form C. 2118.

WAR DIARY
or
INTELLIGENCE SUMMARY.
(Erase heading not required.)

4th Battalion Suffolk Regt (T.F.)

Instructions regarding War Diaries and Intelligence Summaries are contained in F.S. Regs., Part II. and the Staff Manual respectively. Title pages will be prepared in manuscript.

Place	Date	Hour	Summary of Events and Information	Remarks and references to Appendices
TROISDORF	23.5.19		Conference under Company Commanders re arrangements of week.	
	24.5.19		Working party to R.E.s. Corps at critical P.P.C. Corps Working Party H.P. S.s. Batt: Cricket Match V 103 Field Amb. Result 4-2/H.K.R. 58 runs	Objects in
	25.5.19		103 Field Amb: 151 runs. Church parade in Palm Salma at 11.00 hours.	2.5.4. attached
	26.5.19		Company training. Working party H.P. S.s.	
	27.5.19		Company training. Working party to R.E.S.	
	28.5.19		A Coy. Found Guard on Broamuel H.Q. 1.Sgt. 1/L/Cpl. 1 Dmr. 6 ptes. B Coy. Found Army Ammunition Dump Guard Sgt=GBURC. Lent to Corps. Lent G Rocks at H.Q. 1 Sgt. 2 Cpls. 24 Ptes. 48ptes. Working party to R.E.s. Bath: Cricket Match V 92 Field Ambulance. (Bon Temps)	
	29.5.19		Company training	
	30.5.19		Company training	
	31.5.19		Company training Battn: Cricket. D Coy. V Rest of Battn.	

L.Ottors
Lt. Colonel,
Commanding 4th Bn. Suffolk Regt.

BATTALION ORDERS.
by
Lieutenant Colonel G.C.STUBBS, D.S.O.
Commanding 4th Battalion Suffolk Regiment.
In the Field.

Copy No. 10   May 25th 1919.

1. In the event of the Germans refusing to sign the Peace Terms the Armistice will be broken off, three days notice being given. At the end of three days the Allies will advance. The date of advance is called 'J' day. The earliest date that 'J' can be is Monday May 26th. In the event of negotiations it may be any subsequent day.

2. On 'J' minus one day the Division will concentrate as close to the perimeter as possible in four Brigade Groups.
   The Battalion belongs to the 3rd Brigade Group consisting of:-
   3rd Infantry Brigade. (Brigadier-General C.B.HIGGINSON. C.M.G.
                                                           D.S.O.)
   160th Brigade R.F.A. and 1 section D.A.C.
   208 Field Company R.E.
   34th Bn. M.G.Corps. (less 2 companies).
   4th Bn. Suffolk Regiment.
   103rd Field Ambulance.
   No. 1 Coy. Divisional Train.

   This Group will concentrate in the Area, NEUNKIRCHEN - SEELSCHIDE - BIRK.

3. On 'J' day the 3rd Brigade Group will advance via MUCH to FORST. On 'J' plus 1 day to NEUSTADT. On 'J' plus 2 days to OLPE. On 'J' plus 3 days to Railway between ALTEN MUNDEN and NEWBRUCK.

4. Officers commanding Companies will make all arrangements to move at short notice.
   (a) Dress: Marching order with 120 rounds S.A.A. 1 Blanket per man will be rolled in bundles of 10 and will be carried on lorries.
   (b) All surplus kit will be taken in to Company Stores.
   (c) Each Company will detail 2 men as guard for their stores.
   (d) H.Q. and Transport stores will be stored in the Recreation Room at the Factory.

5. Two Platoons of 'A' Company will rejoin Battalion on orders from Battalion H.Q.

6. "D" Company will remain at HERKENRATH and be prepared to join Battalion leaving surplus stores under a guard of 1 N.C.O. and 3 Ptes. at HERKENRATH.

7. All employed men surplus to fighting and administrative H.Q.'s will rejoin their Companies. These men will be notified to Coy. Sgt.-Majors by the Regtl. Sergt. Major.

8. On concentration being orderd, Lieut. KNAPP (now at Divisional School) will report to O.C. Reception Camp to take charge of details arriving from leave.

9. Maps 1/100,000 and 1/200,000 will be issued, and all Officers will study the route and areas mentioned in paras. 2 & 3 and make themselves conversant with the Country and places named.

10. On receipt of these Orders "A" and "B" Coys. will take over their Company tools and detail one man to be in charge permanently.

11. Company Commanders will ensure that all men have two good pairs of socks and that boots are serviceable - that arrangements are made for the storing of all mens' private property.

12. Orders issued on the 22nd instant are cancelled and the above substituted. Further instructions will probably be issued from time to time.

                                                    P.G. Panley
                                                    Captn. & Adjutant.
Distribution overleaf.   4th Bn. Suffolk Regt.

DISTRIBUTION:

Copy No. 1 to 'A'
2   'B'
3   'D'
4   Q.Mr.
5   T.O.
6   C.O.
7   2nd i/c.
8   Spare.
9   War Diary.
10.   -do-
11   File.

Army Form C. 2118.

WAR DIARY or INTELLIGENCE SUMMARY.

(Erase heading not required.)

4th Bn. Suffolk Regiment

4TH BATTALION. SUFFOLK REGIMENT.

Place	Date	Hour	Summary of Events and Information	Remarks and references to Appendices
TROISDORF	1.6.19		Battalion parade for Church in Powder Factory at 1000 hours. 2⁄I. 2nd Highlanders found Bn. Guard. 13th & packed to 13 Coy	
	2.6.19		Company training.	
	3.6.19		King's Birthday. A holiday granted. All ranks were in the cap in commemoration of the Battle of RETTINGEN. Lt. T.R. Googe posted to 53rd R.Sussex Rgt on from 29/5/19 Officers of the Bn. v Red & Bn. at crickets at 10.30 hours	
	4.6.19		Company training. 4th Bn. R.S. Rgt. War Savings Association restarted & affiliated to National War Savings Association.	
	5.6.19		Battalion Parade at 10.00 hours for lecture on "War Savings" by the Commanding Officer.	
	6.6.19		Company training. Cricket Match: Battn. v 15th / 13th Lancashire Fusiliers	
	7.6.19		Company training.	
	8.6.19		Battn. paraded for Church in Powder Factory at 1100 hours. Capt. & Qr. T. Scott joined Battn.	
	9.6.19		Company training. Route march 09.30 hours. Route — SIEGLAR — SPOICH.	
	10.6.19		Battn. Parade for Qualifying period for leave fixed at 3 months.	
	11.6.19		Company training.	
	12.6.19		Company training. Lieut G. Roskruge transferred from 13th to A Coy. Battn.	
	13.6.19		Company training. Cap. Somerville Battn. v 13th/ 13th Lancashire Fusiliers Hockey Match.	
	14.6.19		Company training. Battn. Cricket Match V 53rd / 18th Welsh Regt.	
	15.6.19		Battn. paraded Church in Powder Factory at 1000 hours. War Savings Total to date £6, 4, 5	

G.H. Watts, Lt. Colonel
Commanding 4th Bn. Suffolk Regt

Army Form C. 2118.

4TH BATTALION.
SUFFOLK
REGIMENT.

WAR DIARY
or
INTELLIGENCE SUMMARY.

(Erase heading not required.)

H.Q. 4th. Suffolk Regt (4 Bn 77)

Instructions regarding War Diaries and Intelligence Summaries are contained in F.S. Regs., Part II. and the Staff Manual respectively. Title pages will be prepared in manuscript.

Place	Date	Hour	Summary of Events and Information	Remarks and references to Appendices
TROISDORF	16.6.19		Company training. Cricket match. Batt. v R.K.R.	
"	17.6.19		Company training. Cricket match at Bonn. Batt. v 1st Border Regt. Committee elected to represent Batt. nat Savings Association. Chairman Lieut Col. G.C. Stubbs D.S.O. Treasurer Lieut E.L. Hope. Sec. C.Q.M.S. W.R. Jephson	
"	18.6.19		Coys under Coy arrangements. Reports to Rohr turn Bahn.	
HEISTER	19.6.19		Batt moved to ALTENRATH AREA at 07.15 hrs. Batt. attached to 3rd Brigade Group for all operations in event of German not signing Peace.	
"	20.6.19		The Batt paraded at 06.55hrs. In Brigade Route march. Move of march shown. B.A. & Coy Transport. An Alfresco Concert at 18.00 hrs.	
"	21.6.19		Batt Parade for Church Service at 10.00 hrs. Football Away v B Coy at 18.00 hrs.	
"	22.6.19		Company training (Advance Guards) Football 1 Coy v H Coy, C v H, D v A.	
"	23.6.19		Coys under Coy Commanders. 1st Home Leave Party proceeded on leave.	
"	24.6.19		Batt paraded for work in Range at Bruckhausen. Cancelled owing to hot Day.	
"	25.6.19		Batt paraded for work in Range at Bruckhausen. Batt. Sentrs under Lt Bailey	
"	26.6.19		Batt paraded for work in Range at Bruckhausen. Batt Sentries under Lt Bailey. Annual Leave opened £136.4.5.	
"	27.6.19		No Parade. Owing to het day.	
"	28.6.19		Batt paraded for work in Range at Bruckhausen. CRE visited Range. All Officers attend lecture by Command Officer. Subject. Infantry & M.G. Force Signal at 15.50 hrs.	
"	29.6.19		Batt parade for Church. at 10 o'c's. Battle accrued the victory T.O.	

#353 Wt. W2544/1454 700,000 5/15 D. D. & L. A.D.S.S./Forms/C. 2118.

Lt. Colonel,
Commanding 4th Bn. Suffolk Regt.

Army Form C. 2118.

4TH BATTALION.
SUFFOLK
REGIMENT.

No.............
Date............

WAR DIARY
or
INTELLIGENCE SUMMARY.

(Erase heading not required.)

Instructions regarding War Diaries and Intelligence Summaries are contained in F. S. Regs., Part II. and the Staff Manual respectively. Title pages will be prepared in manuscript.

4th Bn. Suffolk Regt (?)

Place	Date	Hour	Summary of Events and Information	Remarks and references to Appendices
HEISTER.	30.6.14.		The Battn. less 2 Coys will proceed to TREISDORF at 0h.25m. Starting Point Junction of Roads at present Bivouac Hd. Qtrs. ROHM.R. ALTENRATH. on right bank of RIVER 79/2R. Order of March.Bound. 4t Qr- B,- Hd.Qrs Transport.	

P. White
Lt. Colonel.
Commanding 4th Bn. Suffolk Regt.

Army Form C. 2118.

4TH BATTALION.
SUFFOLK REGIMENT.
4th Bn Suffolk Regt (T.F.)

WAR DIARY
INTELLIGENCE SUMMARY.
(Erase heading not required.)

Instructions regarding War Diaries and Intelligence Summaries are contained in F.S. Regs., Part II. and the Staff Manual respectively. Title pages will be prepared in manuscript.

Place	Date	Hour	Summary of Events and Information	Remarks and references to Appendices
TROISDORF	1.7.19		Companies are placed at the disposal of the O.C.Coys. Maj. R.F.S. Liddiard assumes Command of 1st Battalion from July 1st/19 during the absence of Lieut Col Cadell D.S.O.	
"	2.7.19		Companies are placed at the disposal of O.I.Cs Coys. 2nd/Lt W. Atkinson joined the Batt. from 51st Yorkshire Regt. M.G.C.R. R.S.M. Ready (from 11th assumes that of R.S.M.) Cricket match Batt v M.T.	
"	3.7.19		Peace Celebration observed as a General Holiday throughout the Batt - Cross match Batt v ½ Bn Sigal Coy	
"	4.7.19		Companies will parade for Coy Inspection. Physical Drill, Education 2nd lesson assumed under Coy Signal Officers. W.E.H.E. Elliot asgn 4/11/19 vice 2nd/Lt Monro to 2/20 W Coy.	
"	5.7.19		Companies will parade for Coy Inspection. Physical Drill, Education. Cricket match Batt v 1st Heavy Batty R.G.A.	
"	6.7.19		Church Parade. Special Thanksgiving Service. Batt will parade in Wilhelm Strasse at 10.30 hrs. Roman Catholics will parade at the Rectory at 10.15 hrs.	
"	7.7.19		Coys will parade for Coy Inspection. Physical Drill Education. L/Cpl Holt & 12 Privates & 2nd Lieut Jackson M.C. Cpl Boardman M.M. Pte Marshall left with the Batt Colours for Paris to take part in the Victory March & to HK Cricket match Batt v "C" Corps Signal Company (A Coy win) Declared only 41.	
"	8.7.19		Coys paraded as yesterday. Bty made a visit to the Batt. arriving at 11.00 hrs & played the rest of the Batt at Football at 14.30 hrs Result Coy 2 Rest 13.0. Whale left for UK leave. The Batt turned out to march & play to Sir Caesar Regt. Sports.	
"	9.7.19		Coys paraded for Batt at the M.G.C. Barracks. 135 O.R. & 10 officers went for a trip up the Rhine. Lieut Rena Ashwell (concert Party) visits TROISDORF. Capt Redding returned from Leave.	
"	10.7.19		Coys Parade for Coy Inspection, Physical Drill, Education. Cricket match Batt v 209 K.R.R.	

Army Form C. 2118.

WAR DIARY
or
INTELLIGENCE SUMMARY

(Erase heading not required.)

4TH BATTALION.
SUFFOLK REGIMENT.

Place	Date	Hour	Summary of Events and Information	Remarks and references to Appendices
TROISDORF	11.7.19		Coys parade under Coy arrangements. Capt Simpson MOMS left the Battn & went to Hospital. Capt Knight went to Stroppshal. Went to Paris Leave. RSM Read RE 103 PM. L+ thren	
"	12.7.19		Coys parade under Coy arrangements. A Special train in Cologne runs to 1500 GR, 2 will call Above & UK. L+ Ribton Frater & 1 Sgt & 7 ORs went to Paris Leave.	
	13.7.19		The Batt paraded for Divine Service at 10.30 hrs. & after the RC Check.	
	14.7.19		Coys paraded under Coy arrangements. The Ansley Jump party [?raider] came until Aug 6".	
	15.7.19		Coys paraded under Coy arrangements. Practise Cricket match (?Hereford's) v 2nd Bucks XI.	
	16.7.19		Coys parade for Battn. D5 & Coys. Capt Mueller came from Arnhem to 21 CCS Bonn. Cricket match Battn v 5th Bedfordshire Regt. Ribton Frater returned from Paris. Lt Offman went on Leave. 2 Sgts & 15 OR went to the Brussels Empire Leave Club (Going no, weale He sat).	
	17.7.19		Coys parade under Coy arrangements. Medical Inspection to the Battn. 11 orks in Babies	
	18.7.19		Coys parade under Coy arrangements. Lieut Alden's recurrent Ranbuc part offices accorn Hosp. Return at 19.00hrs would further notice. Cricket match at Bonn Battn v 11 Glouces Regt 2 Hills & Thomas [?received rank] Col. Colonel for the Paris Peace March. Capt whine returned from Artillery Course	
	19.7.19		Observed as a General Holiday (E. Stu. S.) Cricket match the Cap. Battn v 5th Lances Regt. two american officer came to breakfast Lost the way to Cas.	
	20.7.19		Church Parade at 11.15hrs in NCC Barracks Roman Catholics paraded at 10.15hrs	
	21.7.19		B Coy working in Arsenal Hurse Show Ground King funeral fired General Guard	
	22.7.19		Laundry 1st Class Army Certificate of Education. B Coy working in Arsenal Hurse Show Ground. Head quarters went to Cann to UK Cricket match Battn v 30t. C Battery.Pol Schutz returning from Leave.	
	23.7.19		Bates added to #.B. HQ Coy. Thirty men of B Coy working on the Horse Show Ground. Fifty men went on a Rhine Trip. The Strong of the Bethnah from Hotel Rutland went authorized Cricket match at Bonn, Batt v Canade Bru. M.T. Coy. Lieut Col Strutton DSO resumed Command of the Battn.	
	24.7.19		Coys under Coy Commander's Arrangements. Racing parties. Amounts Subscribed to the Tpr Saving's Sweep stake tickets S.W to Take = 365.	

WESTMINSTER Schoolley 1215 D.D.&L ADJ.S.S./Forms/C.2118. A (Trgl 213.- 1. Blvy.1286.-13/10. Rcoy/2308.-8-2. M3.Coy.282.-3. O.T.Totl.2185.-7-1.

[signature] Lt. Colonel
Commanding 4th Bn. Suffolk Regt

WAR DIARY
or
INTELLIGENCE SUMMARY.

(Erase heading not required.)

Army Form C. 2118.

4TH BATTALION. SUFFOLK REGIMENT.

4 Batt. Suffolk Regt. (T.F.)

Place	Date	Hour	Summary of Events and Information	Remarks and references to Appendices
TROISDORF	25.7.19.		Coys made Coy arrangements. Inspection by M.O. at 11.30hrs. Battle ex-Prisoners returned from B.R.	
	26.7.19.		The Commanding Officer inspected all Billets, also store rooms. Cricket match Batt v. Coy Bde.	
	27.7.19.		The 13½M attended Divine Service in the Powder factory, at the Recreation Room at 10.00hrs. School for trick riding aug. 2nd. Parrelle. 06.30hrs. S.Antk. 07.00hrs. Breakfast 08.00hrs. Swimming 12.00hr. from 12.30hrs. Retreat 96.00hrs. Cricket match Batt v Lancashire Bn. M.T. Coy. R.P.	
	28.7.19.		Coys made Coy arrangements. B Coy found 3 O.R. to take part at the Brigade Show Sound Lecture at Siegburg at 14.30 hrs to Pay & Mess Books by the Command Paymaster.	
	29.7.19.		Coys made Coy arrangements. B Coy found 3 O.R. on fatigue at the Brigade Show Ground. It. Knapp went on Leave to U.K.	
	30.7.19.		Batts allotted to "A" Bn. H.Q. Coy at M.G.C. Barracks. 3rd R.A. Coy in fatigue at the Swimming Bay Ground. Major Coulh went on leave to U.K. It. Hill returned from Leave. Cricket match Batt v 13 Kings Regt.	
	31.7.19.		No parade after 10.00hrs, then allowed to go to the Industrial Horse Show at Siegburg. 5 Coys Cars over form Herdenrath to Huiden stay. Batt v non 15 Prigs R.E.S. Army in Rhein. open driven. 1st 1st etc etc Cottle & Pair (open Bn). 2nd Major Cauff. Pair (open Bn). 3rd Infantry Transport turnout. Open Horse. Major Carpenter RSO came to Headen stay. All Leave stopped & driven bn.	

C. Shotts Lepper

www.ingramcontent.com/pod-product-compliance
Lightning Source LLC
Chambersburg PA
CBHW081436160426
43193CB00013B/2297